TRAPPED INSIDE MY MIND

7 DIMENSIONS IN BLACK AND WHITE;

POETRY FROM THE PERSPECTIVE OF A SCHIZOPHRENIC

TRAPPED INSIDE MY MIND

7 DIMENSIONS IN BLACK AND WHITE;
POETRY FROM THE PERSPECTIVE OF A SCHIZOPHRENIC

TIMOTHY V. LANE

THIRD EYE PUBLISHING

Red Oak, Texas

TRAPPED INSIDE MY MIND
Published by:
Third Eye Publishing
Red Oak, Texas
voncewaylon@gmail.com

Timothy V. Lane, Publisher and President
Mahogany Byrd, CEO and Associate Publisher
Zharia Ransom, Editorial Director
Yvonne Rose/QualityPress.info, Book Packager

The author may make any part of this autobiography available to organizations that serve any of the following: youth organizations, educational organizations, training programs, cultural studies courses, or libraries upon written request.

ISBN#: 978-0-692-13521-1
Library of Congress Control Number: 2018908268

DEDICATION

This book is dedicated to the following people who without them in my life I wouldn't be who I am today, and this project would not be possible:

First, my parents and creators Luther T. Lane and Vanessa Lane who I owe everything to, my uncle Gregory Carroll, and my aunt Vicky Carroll who suggested that I write a book in the first place that was about ten years ago, it's been a long time coming, but it's finally here now.

I would also like to dedicate this book to my wife's parents Mr. Claude Stanley Byrd and the late Ms. Gwendolyn Byrd, R.I. P, also Mrs. Mary Anne Byrd. I would also like to dedicate this book to Mr. Ronnie Lane and Mrs. Sheila Lane, my uncle and aunt. Also, my uncle and aunt, Mr. Bobby Harris and the late Mrs. Shirley Temple Harris. I would also like to dedicate this book to my aunt Delores Carroll and my sister Timeekah Lane who has been there every step of the way since I've been going through this.

My wife Mahogany Byrd Lane who words cannot describe how I feel about her, she is the foundation and inspiration for the material in this book.

My aunt, Franceila Graves. My grandparents, the late Carey Carroll and Sarah Carroll (still living), the late Luther T. Lane Sr. and the late Bernice Lane R.I.P.

Last, but not least and most importantly, I dedicate this book to my three kids - Zharia. Timille, and Autumn - for they are the reason this is possible.

R.I.P. Larry Carroll, Cheryl Carroll, and Rita Carroll; also R.I.P. Sharlon Rogers and Pamela Cooks.

ACKNOWLEDGEMENTS

Dr. Bobby Hemmitt, whose YouTube videos were very informative; Dr. John L. Johnson, whose book "The Black Biblical History" was very educational; John G. Jackson, whose book "Christianity Before Christ" also was very educational; Dr. Booker T. and Dr. Oyibo, whose YouTube videos basically proved what I have been saying this entire time.

CONTENTS

INTRODUCTION

Most of you may not be familiar with mental illness but if you are someone who suffers or know of someone who suffers from mental illness this is a project that proves that people who are affected by this tragic condition can create something of substance, that they can be more than just their illness. My college education was interrupted by this disease, but I am not one to be ignorant and lack knowledge. I self-educated myself on what was happening to me, the disease itself, and most importantly I educated myself on the science of the universe, the Earth, and how it relates to me as a human being and I still have much to learn. Being that schizophrenia is now understood to be a chemical imbalance in the brain, I have been brought back to the ancient mysterious world and teachings of Kemmitt (Egypt), thus where the term "chemical" originates. With this project, if nothing else, I wanted to prove that people with mental illness can be functional and productive in society. First, I want to start by saying the universe is made of melanin and the pineal gland inside the brain (responsible for supernatural phenomenon) produces melanin. To those who are not aware of the symptoms of paranoid schizophrenia in which I was diagnosed with 20 years ago, I suffer from audio and visual hallucinations. I hear voices and have visions.

Schizophrenia was known in ancient times as demonic possession. People with this condition suffer from what is called religious fanaticism, for those of you who do not know what that is, that is when you are obsessed with religion. Being that, I come from a Southern Baptist Christian background, I was always under the impression that God was separate from the organic. I believed my salvation was in the sky, but through this entire ordeal that has lasted for the past two decades, I have come to realize that my salvation lives within. Sure enough, the sky is my salvation. In scripture, the sky like the oceans, are the waters. Waters are multitudes and nations, and multitudes are voices, I am 38 now, when I first heard them I was 19. I was at a point of time in my life when I was on a quest to abandon my childhood, from a boy to become a man. I was searching for God, but more obsessed with the kingdom of Heaven. I came home one night, after a night of intoxication, to an empty house when I was living with my grandparents who were out of town at the time in Los Angeles visiting my great uncle. I remember plainly that I had cut all the television sets off in the house before I left that day. When I came in the house and I went into my room, the television was on. It was on Channel 58 TBN, the Christian Network. There was a pastor on tv named John Haggee, he was discussing the book of revelations and describing the events therein. I had never read the Book of Revelations. So I decided to pick it up and read. As I read, I began to hear the voices speak to me. Saying to me "You see, you are the reason. It's you. You are God." These were seven familiar voices, family members. A host of uncles and aunts, my mother, and my beloved eldest cousin on my mother's side of the family. Then, when I approached Revelations chapter 19, at the age of 19, I heard an eighth voice, it was a female. Her name was Heaven. It was a memory of what was once one of the most enchanting of feelings, a memory of an old childhood classmate of whom at the time I wondered where she was. I eventually sought out to find her, and I did years later. But only after I met the woman who I'm with now and whom is the mother of my children. These eight voices, the seven on one side of my brain and the eighth on the other work together to keep me enticed and enthused about living life. The whole quest was to find God, and God is family. That is something, at that time, that I was yearning for, a bride and kids. Revelations chapter 19 speaks of the Messiah and his bride the kingdom of Heaven. Heaven to me is incarnated into every female being and so if Heaven is a woman, then God must be a man, and this is the mentality I took with me throughout my life, ever since I met Heaven all those years ago at the age of 3 years old. Through my waiting and searching for the kingdom of Heaven I have endured emotional and spiritual torment, so to the point where I have no feeling now. I have sunken deep into the abyss, the lowest of lows if you believe in the spiritual Hell, believe me, I am here now. My late grandmother Mrs. Lane used to say that it can't be dark forever eventually the sun has to shine, well this is me shedding light on my dark life. I have cursed God and I have cursed Heaven because I wanted it so bad. But more than that, I wanted to know if Heaven and the seven voices that I hear, (which are the equivalent to the seven days of the week, the seven spirits of God, the seven seas, the seven stars, and the seven nations) wanted me. Remembering that the waters are multitudes and the multitudes are voices. These voices continuously coach me and plead with me not to commit suicide. They inform me and remind me of who I am as in "The great I am." They give me a sense of purpose here. I struggle to take my medication because the medication is designed to destroy the voices and if the voices are gone I probably will be too. I get no rest from the voices I hear them 24 hours, seven days a week, it's enough to drive anybody insane. The voices reveal to me these things about the origins of man and God. I research and study and find that what they were telling me is the truth. I have come to view this as something more scientific than spiritual. I have come to realize that I am different from most and that I have access to a portion of my brain that most people don't. I have not yet learned how to use this to my advantage, but then again, maybe this is the beginning. I started writing poetry 20 years ago inspired by the memory of Heaven, the same time I started hearing the voices. This book is a compilation of what I have been hearing inside of my head for the past 20 years. It is a book of emotions and I dedicate this book to my wife, the love of my life, Mahogany, my parents, Luther Jr. and Vanessa Lane, my three daughters, Zharia, Timille, and Autumn, my sister Timeekah Lane, my niece Sanaa, and my grandparents, Carey and Sarah Carroll. Rest in Peace Carey Carroll, and Luther Sr. and Bernice Lane, rest in peace. I hope that you receive this with deep interest into the mind of someone who suffers from this condition. And

I hope that this project if not anything else at least proves that there is some intelligence in the mind of a schizophrenic. I really hope to help someone. Thank you for your purchase and I hope you are fulfilled and inspired. Sincerely,

Timothy V. Lane

PART ONE:
POETRY FROM MY MIND

Morphing written in 2011

I am an embodied being, but I have the ability to change what I am; this being into some other matter that you may not recognize, or even know if I am. If I am something that you could be seeing or believing to exist in the state of the physical, but inside of this embodied structure lurks something similar to the spiritual. An energy thought to be infinite in its abilities. Able to change motion, change in motion, and motion to change all that stems from our brains and reign a kingdom of stability, in whatever body that takes me. Whether in human form or the form of our galaxies, I morph into something greater than the hater of my physicalities. Something that is the core existence of spirituality and life beyond what we know the M.E.S.T. to be. Matter, Energy, Space, and Time, I may just escape from thee. The violent past of how our lives came to be, turmoil in the   creation in which our imaginations reveals instability, upon the planet, in what we conceive as our God, damn it. If it isn't, then it's feeling damn it, because of this concealing of the infinite in its brilliance of how we continue to keep living in the midst of all of the destruction and killing of lives across the map and planet. There is no need to stand and clap, for what, and give praise because now we see the end of days, our knowledge has overlapped in its ways in a sense that we cannot see past our creation. So hence, we forget our infinity and placed limits on our physical state and because we continue to hate ourselves for not being true to the other 90 percentile of our being held above and beyond the physical me and you. We too will consume all that is physical and carnal until there is nothing but a thought left of another truth. What am I morphing into?

Dimensions 2011

In this dimension we have consciousness with the makeup of three beings: mind, body, and soul. Which one of these three can lay claim to the beginning of me. What am I seeing if I, my being as a whole my sight cannot behold. What I hold maybe something that can exist in any dimension. With this, my true intention is to choose from two sides, the matter of my substance, and the masses within my eyes. As well as my pride is being exposed each time that I feel, my anatomic make-up is more than the suppose of this thought that you take up, from this release of this notion. As deep as an ocean, I open my mind beyond this dimension and embrace all ways of transmission of brain waves from our mental into the subliminal. I secure my survival even after the demise of the physical. For the thought is an instrumental, a confidential reminder of my infiniteness, and to pretend that this exists. My theta is more than physical matter, but for what happens after it, I do not cease to explain; that the rapture will come when we all begat one collective understanding of our universe and our bodies, souls and energies generated from our brains from when we planned this. This consciousness is the hereafter, what I know to be true and sane in this third dimension. The ability to choose is the other two that we cannot seem to explain or evade, possibilities which could be made just in case it is not safe to leave this place. Since should a cataclysmic event take place upon the body of the Earth, I know of a fourth dimension that we will come to understand and I know to be of great worth. The general belief that we govern our own thought patterns expanding out into the great wide open. The galaxy's will is ours. Our bodies, some of us are one with all that we can hope and feel, only to sublime through the desires of carnal pleasures. Due to adrenaline increasing in flow, our senses are heightened and are inclined to the points of forever. This heats the body, soul, and mind, consuming its physical converting it from its solid state into its vapor. Thus, morphing beyond matter, energy, space, and time, your soul and mine is revealed. This is the rapture that began the end of lying and hating for and to yourself. Infiniteness has now and always been inside the mind. So why are we waiting? Now here is the precision of time, it is the reality of dimensions. These are mine I'm creating.

The Potential That I See 1996

With all that I can see in me, I can see in the world too. With all that I believe in me, I can believe in all of you, to all of God's people. I bring this message sent from Heaven above. If you battle with all Satan's evil, the greatest weapon is to continue to love. For us, to love and just to believe, is the knowledge to our children that we as young angels need to leave. Yesterday, I was full of joy observing everything around that I could see. I possessed a deep passion for this world, a love for all that only God has found in me. Today, my joy is lost in oceans of doubt for hope of my dreams and my goal, to bring out of the potential in everyone, so I pray to God to release what's inside of my soul. To define the word potential, one's undeveloped capability, to believe in God and goodness is essential, remember, we all possess that ability.

Potential today, for my family I pray, to think highly of the young who believe, because to Satan the young are easy prey and without your encouragement, their faith will deceive. To my lady, the love of my life, this is the potential that I see. Your fascination with the heart I possess and to bring out the goodness in you that was created in me. For tomorrow, in the event of my demise. I will die for a principle because I showed love by opening up my eyes. And for tomorrow, continue to believe that you can succeed and if you're one who gambles with faith, believe in the potential that I see.

Excuse Me Ms. 1997

Excuse me, but can I get to know you and let you see what I have inside, my desire that I possess to express this admiration that I tried to hide? Will you allow me to show you the different reasons for which I live? Things in you that I see strengthens me, and with my spirit is the thanks that I give. I thank God for granting me with this chance, this opportunity to bring to you what I feel. I hope that you can acknowledge my effort and see that my personality is real. I know this may seem all of a sudden, a little somewhat just out of the blue, but there are things that live within me that could be brought out by what lives within you. This is not a proposal of a relationship of any kind. I just want to see what we can bring to each other, who knows what we both may find? You see with every person that I meet, there is something which holds my concern. There are many things that I would like to teach, and there are things that I would like to learn. I first noticed you back in September, that's when all of this really began and now with the start of this new semester, I just want to become your friend. Look into what may I bring. See the reason as to why I strive, and if you are ever troubled with anything then come see ma at 115. In time you will come to see, that what I speak can be held true. Hello, my name is Timothy. Excuse me Miss, but can I get to know you?

My Soul is an Alien... 2010

Contemplating on the emotion of hating, I wonder about where we have been. It is a war on humanity, so easily life can dispense. There is something that is determined to destroy man and mankind forever, leaving our vessels desolate and empty without life and our energy exposed out into the open and blind, waiting for another chance to experience that right, we may never. Why? Is that their right? They inhibit our beings and make us beings their kind. Our carnalities thrive off insight. What if we are not meant to be embodied beings in flesh? What if we were meant to be of an infinite state of mind. So now there is a war on mankind. Probably because we have the ability to choose, which begat our three-dimensional world in all of space., because there was something not trustworthy of the other two. Your soul or your flesh. Which one is the real you? We were never meant to be made human, but we are for a reason and the reason was to consume and rule you. Who is that? Thus, what you are after the combination of the two. A third being. The war between them is centered around you. Mankind wants to destroy your soul because it is alien, an extraterrestrial energy that can inhibit bodies and can destroy you, in infinite ways or give eternal life and they can erase that right for misbehaving. All of these things can erode time upon your flesh and end your days. Is this another way to destroy man, DEATH? Just to get to the power I have to see this? Who is the enemy? Who is trying to end consciousness in this entity? My soul or my flesh. Who is trying to save or destroy humanity? Is it alien, or is it human for me to test?

Psych Out 2010

I might not be this, what you can see. I might not be this, what you can hear. I might not be this in which these words speak. If I could psych myself out and cling to the thought of my being, being brought to the realization that I may not even be, I wonder how long it would take for me to realize what is the make of this contemplation and how does my imagination make me. The psych out will leave no doubt in whatever we choose to believe. That when we believe to the fullest of our potential and we are psyched out, we are outside of our bodies and mental and beyond the physical and natural laws of science and nature and out beyond our third dimensional. In a place where we govern our own routes that are to be. When dealing with the powers of the psyche, destiny and fate both or not the holders of the mighty. There is no destiny or fate when a will is imposed, only the suppose of the extraordinary that is instilled into that other possibility. Those who choose to defy all laws of the galactic, in this state will never fold, and are extremely close to achieving the fantastic. The balance of good and evil on every level will unveil in everything, stability. At last it is within my reach. Everything is me, if I psych myself out and believe this to be. Who can defeat what I aim to be with this thought process that came to me? Wait, is this even me? Do I even live in this century? Is there even time in a deity? Oh shit, what was this even about? Oh, my bad, yeah, the psych out.

Mother's Day 2009

You are my conscious any notion of the kingdom comes from you. You are the energy that forms my physical trues. And I would not think it weren't for the two, your soul which is my Heaven, your flesh, which is me. Forever I as a man will be one with you. Well I know this to be true. If for whatever reason you shall ever stop thinking then I will cease to exist in you. Maybe if I was God, I could see at your Zenith reaching the best of your potential but since I'm probably not, I think it's time for us to realize what you mean to it, the Earth, your seed and my mother, and yourself meditation upon your salvation will lead us to another dimension, in which our insight and wisdom begins a whole new knowledge, a realm of a whole new might. A physiological explosion of new energies vibrant and powerful, giving off bright, golden, light. Infinite choices from life's most pleasant of all the emotions we feel moving all in one rhythmic motion just your devotion to us is more than what we needed to reveal. As I reveal the way to the gold city is through our minds once we conceal the only way into the next realm, in time, preservation, conservation of what has given us life. Mother nature has taken too much strife, and we are only going to win inside our minds when we realize that we care-take over the Earth as if it were our seed, our need to nurture our quality and quantity of time is conceived through what we believe about our ability to continuously incline. Mother, Oh Mother of the Earth, my child, I hope that you see your importance to this, your worth and connection to this style. It is the lifestyle of deity, you live it and your undeniable love represents it, which is why it continuously illuminates the best of me. I love you. Happy Mother's Day.

I Must Say Thank You, 1997

Because you went out of your way to give me the chance to learn about myself, and a chance to learn how to pray. I must say thank you, for all the time you gave to realize as to why I look within, because when I express I know that I'm saved. You see, to bring out what's inside is the only way for me to be true. My greatest fear are the feelings that I hide, because I'm not sure where they will lead to. Most of the time, I'm not even able to show the reason why I had too much faith in the things that helped my dreams to grow, and most of my time I spend lost in visions of hope, that one day I may speak all that my emotions preach, because if I don't, I will never be able to cope. Every chance I get to let someone know how I feel, I see that as a gift from God letting me know that he is real. We all know that life is a battle, but it is not with what's in this world, we fight to learn and teach about our souls, that is the beauty of every boy and girl. But now, I wonder if I have been led to live in my own death, because my words drown in this ocean of feelings that I have felt. I am on a quest to leave my childhood and become a man, but the first thing that I must do, is to get you to understand. My spirit I seem to no longer recognize. I became so caught up with what I am and what I'm not, so caught up in trying to analyze. And now, I give what is left of me, hoping that you can help me find the potential I once was blessed to see before I run out of time. With all that God sees in me, I hope that you may see too. Through one another, today we both believed and that's why I must say thank you.

Financial Collapse 2011

We are evolving into a world where finances don't matter. Think of the disaster, a place where 10 million, a 100 million, or even a billion dollars meant nothing to nobody, not even you. Then what would you be seeking from here on after. A place where wealth is gauged by trust, and there was no urge to deceive or corrupt another because of lust. Could you survive a life that tough, if you knew that the second you began to doubt, your vitals slowed to the point to where you were on your way out. How strong, then would trust and faith be and what would life really be about.

This is the concept of the financial collapse, the demise of the mighty dollar, the very thing that we need to survive; what we thought life was really about. And so, survival of the fittest goes. As their aim is to lay claim on your soul. Reducing the value of our nation the dollar into nothing as a whole. And they will have us working for nothing as they know the culmination of the Euro is taking control over the Eastern portion of the globe. Once trade and industry are controlled by this merge between the pound and the dollar in the form of a chip in which without you couldn't buy or sell anything. You heard of this prophecy before in Rev. Chapter 13 v 17. Save they had the mark of the beast or the number of his name, your soul. This new method of trade and industry will be the downfall of this once great nation as we know it, simple and plain. This introducing more control over the people the end of capitalism and to console you with this new kind of captivation, a sequel with a deadly intention from a new kind of evil, either we accept this transformation of this financial presentation or perish in our ignorance to change and adapt to the situation.

We are headed for Globalism where everyone, worships the same way, and where everyone is conditioned and programed to live a certain way. They are introducing global control over financial, economic, or religious institution and transaction everywhere. There is no solution or action that we can take, the time is here, the time is now. This was constructed to wake you up, it was not meant to scare. We must come together as one, one world, one government, one faith, one covenant, one leader, one sound. It is the NEW World Order. In this order we are bound. So now it happens, this is the reality of the financial collapse.

Mind Over Matter 2010

My mind is the matter. When someone asks what is the matter? The matter is everything, every conscious, whatever the matter is. I'm on it. In a way that you could believe in the supernatural, that next dimension is my intention to go beyond that rapture beyond the entire creation, and implant my own plan of extra-terrestrial outside this third dimensional imagination that we see, this is the matter with me to be one with everything until all things become me, and I am no longer the matter with the will of the galaxy. Tell me, what is the matter? What is the matter with my mind, it doesn't matter, what is the matter with that matter is that which occupies space in the visible world as opposed to spirit or mind? Mind is spirit, spirit is life, which begets matters of all kind, and all kinds of matters alike. The matter is with my mind, but not over me. For I with my eyes can physically see.

It matters not to me if you believe and see in 3D. The Angel on one end and the devil in on the next, we are in between the two begetting a third option in the text. What governs the three is what matters in the mind. So if it is to you then it is. I don't know, it just is. So why does it matter? It matters because this is my mind.

Mind Over Matter II: State of the Abyss 2010

Matter is everything. But, what would matter be without me, as I am imagining. This universe, this world, and this consciousness. What would be it be if I couldn't taste, smell, hear, feel, or see? Something is happening. Why does it seem like I have left me? I still hear little, though no feeling or sight has embraced me, and whatever it is that I hear, it's all what I have already known to be. Family, friends, places, loved ones, and all those who never knew it. Who or what are they to me? Energy; the energy of life's memory. However, no longer in my mind or physical body, my soul lives on through the memory of all of those that I encountered and excited. I was excited, when I saw, felt, tasted, smelt, and heard. But now, what's left of my life is now death, and I can still hear a few words. Could this energy of my memory from those who knew Tim be enough to extract life from those words? Then I could hear them clearly and get a vision. I am imagining what I hear, a vision of what I already know. A vision of life and enough to excite the five senses that I, the fifth element can feel, the beginning of ether, the truth. For the fifth world age of a five-stage world cycle is transitioning. We have been through Earth, wind, water, and fire already now. The fifth element Ether will make your soul burn slow this is that something that we have been missing. The definition, the clear sky, the upper regions beyond the clouds, in other words, all of the things that make you smile. A kind of substance formerly thought to fill all space and act as a medium for transmission of waves between dimensions as well I send these waves from my brain even after my life, life can still say it feels my pleasures and pains. But Ether, my real intention will reveal my sane. And at life's end a memory will remain. This is the energy that can give life erase death and sickness and pain.

This is a cerebral connection to pull all living things together generated inside of the mind and brain. Would we know life if we did not know it existed? Time would condition you, condition you to keep living. So, as we leave, the fourth world of fiery destruction and enter Ether, the fifth world of peace, it is peace of mind, body and soul, it is eternity to say the least. This is me and everything and everything that I see. Matter is everything and everything that makes me. My mind is an illusion, but it is everything that I can feel, and what I make of it, it may be. My mind is the universe, that is how I got over me.

The Cross 2012

The four sides represent the four dimensions. For we live in the third to what controls us, something in a hominoid form which maybe the reason to the speed of our development in which we heard at first of how we were born. Spoken word from whence we first learned to speak handed down generation to generation before writing came to be of worth. Our beginning can be traced as far back to ancient extra-terrestrials. Whose technology was far beyond ours now, resided here on Earth. In this dimension we have other beings other Gods in which is who they are called because we don't understand, that control the physical beings plant and animal life, namely man. The next, the creators of universes, galaxies, stars, and planets, and control these things and the beings who control and inhibit the dimension over us here. Which is why it is clear, to lean not to your own understanding.

But then science has now discovered a fourth, no longer just three in all of the M.E.S.T. to be. Matter, energy, space, and time. This fourth dimension is beyond that. And energy that is infinite and can resurrect life into the sublime. Given to you from the creator, but not of your physicality but of your mind. This is the cross into, back, and beyond time. A reference to your soul and mine. The reason why he paid the cost. So that we can understand the science of why we are lost. The ignorance and oblivious to the fact that there is a center to all creation. That infinite state, to which we speak our deliverance to the truth. Whichever of those four sides of the cross is our salvation. There will come a time where we will not be bound by the physicalities of our imagination, planets, stars, galaxies, constellations. We will come to find that we are the matter and in the realization of that will morph us beyond that contemplation and into something else, another form of life will cross over into the amazing. A place where flesh does not exist, just the energy of mind. The cross beyond time.

The Cross II 2016

At the cross there will be salvation but not because of the story you remember. For we have been in the dark over valuable information, lost to us, but made available to those in a certain financial bracket and that which you couldn't attain unless you are a member. I am coming back to truth. 360 degrees of knowledge and wisdom is the proof. For the cross is just a mathematic and scientific more than spiritual representation of what is truth. The cross represents death to that one which lacks knowledge of self, to resurrect our mental back into the subliminal one, the reality of resurrection, coming full circle 360 degrees back into the source. Of course, the source of all life, carbon is the only way life can evolve and that we are doing at a rapid pace. This is amazing grace and something we should force. The makeup of the carbon atom, six protons, the matter, six neutrons, the transmitters, and six electrons, the energy and spiritual. This is why black lives matter because we are the source of this black liquid substance in the midnight sky, our bodies, are rooms in one big mansion we live in. The universe is a direct link to the black man through this liquid carbon. You ask why I write this, well here's why, here's what they don't want us to know, Carbon 12 is human life, the makeup of a man. It is found in every facet of the known universe, and is in all carbon. 666 is carbon 12 and is the physical makeup of us, existence. We are transitioning. Our cellular structure is transforming into crystalline our bodies are becoming electric, solar powered by the sun and our souls. All plant, animal, and human-life is mutating because of a release of solar energy from the sun back in 2012. From 666 to 616. Six protons, one neutron, six electrons. This transformation is known as carbon seven, the 47th chromosome will transform black people into the powers of Heaven and Hell. We will be mutating from men to GODS exploring hyper-dimensional levels of consciousness and thought, a new earth, a new heaven, and our bodies will act as copper does, when controlling electromagnetic fields. The powers don't stop. This is all real. The study of melanin is the study of Alchemy. It is also black magic and sorcery. The knowledge of transforming the particles in the body, or the soul as well as the universe, into gold, because gold is the greatest conductor of energy and electricity. Releasing the knowledge is not hard for me, it is the will of the inner sun or soul. For these words many lives have paid the cost, and their bloodshed is the reason why I carry my cross, and so as our story goes.

Amen {schyzin} 2011

I am who, amen, who am I? I am that, I am the great, I am. I am a man. If you understand the plan is to increase the need for life to come to the deceased if you believe in the light of the prince of peace to reveal stability in AMEN and the cosmic path in which we've come to understand and believe. The darkness is a prince immense in all the land as we blindly search our way through this universe it is, what is hidden that makes the motive for my search unforgiven by the creator of the curse to the children who are protected by the son of man. This is why we are still living. As sure as our sun shines on the sand I can see my flesh is as dark as he can, who am I then to he and then who's he to me, AMAN, AMEN, AMAN. I'll say it once again this is me, RA was I just like you born to be condemned because they can't accept the fact that we are him, and you are me, a light embodied in the darkness of them. I close my eyes but can still see. I'm seeing them and me or we could be seeing him. Open up your mind and we could be free in him, or why not divide the limbs of the knowledge tree and free me. Release me so I can go and see what it was and why you would not bow down to me causing me to sin. Back when Ethiopia was just a gem; I knew I had to have Ham. He Is black as I am, you and me. So why we look into the dark. We can now see that HAM was not the evil part that we digested in time, but the father at the heart of what we tested that's why we have blessings and pray for a better brethren you and me which is the only way that we can be free of testing, unsure of who was at the fountainhead of civilization, well here is a truth for your contemplation, am of AdHAM means Ham, Ham means Lord, and Lord HAM. HA in Ham means Home. The name

Ham scripturally has been used to describe this world, this dome, people, places and things, besides its original meaning, it means black. As I am, and I am AMAN I mean. For it seems, the name also adopted other definitions and dreams such as dark as this universe, ebony, sunburned, chocolate, and brown as my flesh, this Earth. I found that AM is even universally linked to all ancient deities, as in our Egyptian history which shows in our prayers to AMEN. AMEN King of Kings GOD of GOD praised thee AMAN in form of flesh AdHAM, for it is as I am, the great I am. AdHam Father and Judge of all nations whether be in light our darkness for it is in him and him only in which we will be led to light and contemplation, spark this might this train of thought and insight into all civilization and realize that in the hymns to AMEN we often read that he is hidden to his children, and hidden to gods and men and all nations. AMEN-Ra was associated with the primeval abyss, gods in the creation of the world, and all that is in it. He is the darkness, so how is it that we still worship him? The answer is easy AdHam was banned from grace because AMAN was greedy. It was all about beauty. The name Ham was praised in ancient times, and was viewed as divine. The Ethiopians and Egyptians called their father "HAM, AMEN", or "AMEN-

RA". Thus transforming our whole demeanor and state of mind leaving us embodied in flesh and becoming a light with a might of a whole new meaning, time. The Hebrews pastured the name Ham as a suffix of the dreamin. Eloham the same as Elohim, since the Hebrew letter "I" was interchangeable with 'A". The ancients also called Eloham, "I Am" check Ex. 3:14; John 8:58 the same as Ham (AMEN) it has been that since the sixth day. After this whether you think of me or not, the name also is hidden and his form or similitude is said to be unknown. The throne is where you know I am blinging your thought to Eternity. All for who and from who? AMEN, AMAN that I am and that is all that concerns me.

Trapped Inside My Mind 2011

As I continue to search for wisdom and knowledge as the word says seek the kingdom and you shall find, I realized that the expansion of the heavens and universe is one with my conscious and everything in it is trapped inside my mind. I sit back and think of how it all came together. All matter birth from one atom and then the climatic creation of the sublime, I think I understand now how we are not separate from the forever. Our father Adham is represented by the atom and vice-versa and because of this we are matter, energy, space and time. The meaning of the name Ham means black, scorched and sunburnt just as the sky which carries the stars. My flesh takes on this image dark like this universe, my thoughts are starlight for my insight as Earth revolves around their sparks. Now let's examine who is lord. They say Lucifer is the bearer of light, also known as the prince of darkness. Man was created on the sixth day, the dark atom, Adham is illumination blinging us into existence. We are the ones who started this and this is why we say Amen when we pray. The Amen stems from the word ham in the word Adham also meaning lord. The Hebrew a and o are interchangeable, as well as the d and the t thus merging the atom and Adham together, so you see there is no separation of us from our lord. Secret societies try to perpetuate and make us believe that we are not he, through infiltrating politics and religion not to mention the division of a whole race of people who are the sequel to the dimension. It is not easy but pay close attention and you will see that things are not always what they seem our politics tell us to have faith in a corrupted and evil system, the same system that has murdered most of our chances at redemption, and destroyed any chance of hope for our dream. To be revived and resurrected back into the divine; kings and queens of creation and the foundation for everyone's salvation. I mean, at this point this has to be the only contemplation because of the traps set inside my mind. Traps are set to isolate and deteriorate leaving me stuck with no luck of freedom, making me believe that I am the enemy because of my lack of effort to submit to their will and making me feel that I am the reason. In my father's house are many mansions. The word planet also means wanderer. I am wondering, if this world is thought, how many thoughts will have happenings like this one. What is the meaning of understanding and is the sky really something that we stand under. Religions of the world all originate from the same place masking themselves with man-made traditions to overtake and rule with their intentions of destroying the masses of the people, people of color, in all forgetting the original color of Amens face and the truth about his religions. Oh no, now I'm Schyzin. I hear 7 voices telling me that I am forever living, living forever in another dimension and at the same time as this one. There's an 8th that tells me I am king of these, could this be Heaven? Oh, it was her I forgot to mention. I think so, and so now I am placed, and driven forever. I am hidden as in the great I am. I can say that because mentally, spiritually, and physically I am the makeup of the atom, oh Adham I ask myself why hast thou forsaken thee. They try to make me believe that ZEUS is king instead of me while I am riding this hypocritical Roman-Catholic beast named Christianity. It is as if we are all content to be afraid of being free, embodied, and trapped inside the shackles of the universe. My God, what has happened to me? I have been robbed of all scientific, mathematic, and historic knowledge. I have lost my identity. Maybe I should just blaspheme and exit myself and everyone else who live of the profits of my wealth, in the way of knowing how to navigate through my mind and trying to find the core of my existence before me and the ones who are really mine. They say fuck me and everyone else, so I should say fuck you and everyone else, commit suicide so all of you die. Then you don't exist in me remember I am the universe, one entity all of matter is driven through me. Wait a minute, I'm going to deep. But then Heaven, she speaks she says; listen to me. You are driven forever because of me, I was your thoughts passion, I am your energy, the very beginning, the light that transformed us into matter, the reason why we are expanding and in motion. Go to the book's ending hmmm. Well I'll turn to Rev. Chpt.12 v 1-5, then you'll know exactly for sure and for show who loves you. You ask why. You see read, the woman who bore the man child was me, and you are my Atom. ADHAM I am your EVE. Set to rule all nations with a rod of Iron and caught up to GOD'S throne. Then she says I am your throne please cross Tim, come back home. Then the voices cease. Oh now I see it begins me out of you and then you out of me. So you see, we are everything, so why are forced to believe that we can't have everything when my physicality is just 10% of me. I want back everything that was stolen from my identity. All of the knowledge and wisdom these things are my God-given and the reason why we are living, to inherit this kingdom and rule it without evil intention. From understanding the dynamics of creation to the realization of the illusion of time. I'm thinking of how it can all be mine while traveling through space, I take my place. My grace is trapped inside my mind.

Mother's Day Poem Part II 2012

GRANDMOTHER, MOTHER, AUNT. You are the epitome of what God's kingdom is. Everything about your loving heart is angelic and it is a precious relic in the lives that you have given us to live. I hope and pray that one day my children emulate your nature. From your stern command to your amazing grace, we continue to search for our place as you continue to raise a young nation. It is because of you that we have dreams of being the best, we realize the struggles and sacrifices you made to keep us all together and how you prayed to GOD that we would remember the things that you taught us, because it was through those things in which we would realize how we are blessed. And our dreams did come true. Whether you know it or not Mother, Aunt, Grandmother, our dream is letting you know how we feel about you. At the end of this poem, me and my children prayed that you would reach your full potential through them one day, and if I should fail to show them the way back to grace, they will remember that they gave you this poem on this HAPPY MOTHER'S DAY

Father's Day 2013

FATHER, GRANDFATHER, UNCLE, I can only dream of being the man that you are, the man that you made me to be. Both one in the same as I am created in your image and bare your nature and name, I love you as if you were LORD and I hope to finish this journey you have set before me. You have the strength of a lion and the power and instinct of a tiger when faced with adversity. At first glance they see that you will never fold, from your youthful days until those of your old and that your purpose here is to bring out the best in Meek and me. For the meek will inherit the Earth and the strong will lead as I show my strength in this by saying that you make up most of me. Sometimes, we disagree but I am confident in knowing that you have my best interest, and the only way for me to be free is to accept what you have shown me, and listen to your voice inside of me so I might be loosened of the shackles of this dimension. My true intention, is to make you overjoyed, that your seed succeeds in the same failures of your life that you thought had destroyed portions of your hopes and dreams, and with that said, I am proud to say that I am the son, grandson, and nephew of the king. HAPPY FATHER'S DAY.

To Fight for a Heaven Star 1998

If there is a star in Heaven that with one wish, all of my dreams would come true my 1 wish would be to fight with all of God's might for you. If there is a star in Heaven who could reunite me with the days of my childhood youth, when our bodies sung and souls danced and our play and laughter painted the picture of truth. This is to a Heaven Star who's beautiful gleam never left my eye. Remember as far back as the precious age of 4 & 5, and at 19 I still dream to rise that high. When the season changed you would play a song, and everyone who was in "Heaven's Hood" would all hear it as we all would walk along hoping that if we were good, we would all feel it, and sure as we hoped we would all feel what we all had believed , and that's why we danced so hard as you shined bright throughout the night of the Eve. I remember when you would send down a magical aroma, and we all would look up and you would see our hungry eyes filled with nothing but greed. I never understood why when we'd beg you would turn on us, I guess because you knew there was a whole family to feed, but then when we did receive, it was more satisfaction than one child would ever need, which is why I strive to get high just by smoking on my weed. Yeah, I fight for a Heaven Star, and I guess that's something for me to admit remembering those days "win" me and you had played hide "n" go seek, and I never wanted to be it. I guess that's because I didn't like chasing and no matter how fast I ran, I didn't have the speed to catch. So now my anger to fight is my replacement and with that I can never forget. Yeah, remembering so clearly now, and how we all stood there with our feet planted in that big circle, then asked how many pieces do you wish, then you'd wish hoping it would come back and free you, because that rhyming seems to last forever.

To Fight for a Heaven Star Part II 2002

1st Timothy chapter 6v 12 THE SEQUEL: Fighting the good fight of faith...

To the star in Heaven with all my dreams and aspirations, I have prayed that the fight will be for the throne because the throne seems to be all of my salvation. With all of my faith I have pledged my love for you, and with all of the world's hate, you alleged to be the one whose power was love and alleged to be the one who was true. Without proof I believed that the one who had hatred was hate because of the power of love for the fight was his fate. And without proof I believed that the one who was deceived was deceived because he deceived the one who was inside of him, using the power of faith. But what is faith? Is it really the evidence of the things not seen and the substance of things hoped for? Where is the proof that it brings to fate; the things you need? What is proved from the things you say you live for? To the star which is Christ is it said that you will come like a thief in the night, if so, why should I always be nice when you steal from me, that only gives me a reason to fight. A fight to prove that my faith was true, even if I used it to deceive myself just so I can say I believed in you. What is it in the darkness that makes me believe that I can't see? What is it in the light that always finds a way to blind me? What is it in the heat that makes it so hot I can't stand? What is it in the cold of my soul in which a part of it is so frozen, it brings out the evil in a man? What do I do when Satan wants to crucify me, and you want to burn me? When life takes the form of death and I hear both of your voices come together and say, "Remember what you learned G." In your right hand there are 7 G's who know of the love and faith of the eighth in need. They make him pray for what he desires and with fire all he wants is to be the G.O.D.eed. And as the root of all evil burns smoke to the sky, all he wants to do is hit it and hope that the green in this blue world can ascend him high. High enough to where he can stare Heaven in the eyes, so he can see if he sees himself intertwined with glory and power, dancing with the love of the kingdom inside. Who wonders why evil exists the way that it does? When everyone and every being are searching for an answer and the answer is searching for love. To believe that one day love and an answer will come, and all of the demons will be exercised and released to ascend back to Heaven, from which they really come from. That is the true nature of the fight, to recognize what love really is. To know when love is selfish and to know when love gives. When will love be for me; I have asked myself that question a million times, when will I get back my soul which was stolen from me so it could be reunited with my mind. Together they become a powerful weapon against my enemy, but who is the enemy? Is it me, or the one who says he is a friend of mine? Why should the enemy be me, how do I know it's not the one of whom I speak of in this rhyme? Who is fighting against me trying to keep me from what's rightfully mine; a crown in Heaven. Is it Lucifer or God, one trying to keep me from uplifting her, one trying to keep me from corrupting her, who is trying to keep me from forever…

This is to you Jesus, I ask if you really want me to fight for you, then please by all means and dreams please us. But even though in the battle my heart has been scarred, I still know that my kingdom and my salvation lies in what seems to be an eternal fight, The Fight for the Heaven Star. G.ame O.ver D. evils

The Doctor 2017

Ever since the darkness fell upon my life, she has been there helping me to deal with the hurt, pain and strife. She first met me when I was 19. I said to her in our first meeting that I wanted everything in this universe to just burn up, I didn't care about anything. Then one thing she said to me stood out. She told me she would fight for me and with me like a lioness and that gave me a pride in which I could not give up. My astrological sign is leo, a lion, a king confident and mighty in battle, by her saying that aligned the stars around my mind. Meeting her was destiny as I prepared for the battle of my life and physical and spiritual being. As the voices grew stronger and eventually sunk me into the dark of the abyss, My visits with her were light guiding me towards my mother , the creator of my darkness, I realize my life is this. Talking with my doctor I always feel like that I have prospered. She is always being truthful with me and breaks things down scientifically, spiritually what she knows about the mind can be backed scripturally and my attention is what I offer. For the seed of the universe is the light of the mind and the 7 voices that I hear are just thoughts dispersed into the universe that are mine. No angels or demons controlling my destiny, but instead she has shown that my destiny controls those angels and demons within and in realizing this I have grown. Dedicated to Dr. Inna Kogan.

42

PART TWO:
DON'T BE AFRAID OF THE DARK – THE SECRETS OF MELANIN

7 Letters in Lucifer, 6 Letters in Christ-Holy Hell 2014

The ancient study of melanin is alchemy, study of stones, particles in the body or universe condensed down to one primordial form inside of us and the melanin inside of us is the highest and most potent form it is called the atom or the seed. This was not constructed or meant to scare, or decline you into spiritual despair. This is meant to enlighten you about yourself in which most of us are reluctant and are not aware. This is meant to make us see and believe. I think back to how it all started in the beginning it was the primordial waters of darkness and it was chaotic. In the realm of the goddess Tahyamiyat or Iset or Isis, the Great mother, the Earth before the continental drift, Tahyamiyat, Tah meaning land and Ahmiyat meaning land of Ahmiyat, Isis' (Auset) name translates to mean mother of God and of Heaven. She is also the equal of the Atom-RA or the Amen. Her husband, Osiris reincarnated into her son Osiris-Horus is associated with the sun and resurrection and is depicted as king of forever. Before then in this darkness or chaos before the creation in Heaven, however, there was the primordial realm of the divine feminine that was later on replaced by her seed as she fell asleep. She went into an intermission and the offspring, her child, the younger force of the universe took over. I am crossing that thin line between science and religion so pay close attention as I began my ascension deep to seek the truth and recover. Her seed defeated Isis (Auset) and used her blood to make humans. By using her blood the triple darkness of space to make humans, this is the mystery of what was her blood. It was the primordial cosmic carbon substance 666, 6 protons (the material), 6 neutrons (transmitters), 6 electrons, (the spiritual), carbon or cosh or black substance, acasha, meaning melanin. Her blood was this primordial water or black liquid water. This water, the liquid water separated and caused the oceans, and the other portions are space and in man. Melanin is the GOD particle, the one, true and divine plan of the great mother, which we have a cosmic thirst for water and need for liquids being realistic it is called "something" that is left behind. "We are the mystic. I do remind that this world was created or built on several other primordial worlds that existed before creation. Those worlds that existed before creation was the realm of Isis (Auset) or Tahyamat the great mother which now exist in something left behind in us black people. This is salvation. That something left behind is melanin also called Damiens the sequel. Melanin is the origin of all of which you are taught that is evil. Listen my people, sorcery is alchemy. Everything in the Christian Bible that in which we are taught that is evil is melanin. Damiens, Demon the word Damien comes from the word AMEN which means hidden and Amon RA is the hidden god, hidden in the darkness, the darkness is melanin. You get the word Amon then Amen, then Damien then the word Demon. This Daimonic substance is the something that is left behind. In the beginning was melanin or chaos something that never stops moving. It is called rusa in ancient India. And this rusa is always in the process of change, and change is the order of chaos. It is always in the order of creating a new reality. And when it is embodied and stifled and put into a box, it stops creating and then it grows stronger and then it destroys, that's our actuality. To pinpoint any location of the universe you need the coordinates x, y, and z the three-dimensional realm in which we exist. This means you have two sides in three directions, up and down, side to side, and forward and back; this equals 6. The number of sides on a cube or box. The universe is our reflection. Well, I think outside the box. With no intended direction. That's the way to get back to the true reality. To reach that 7th carbon state in which there is no relation to distance, time, or direction in which you become one with everything within and around you, you sublime into a multidimensional being, I'm believing now that secret box is unlocked. Now I am the protection. Receive this with no rejection. We are the entity that is the divine. THE GREAT EMMACULATION. Melanin is unlimited and absolute power, it is the reason why we shine. At the core of every star, there is this carbon substance called melanin. At the core of every being there lies melanin. Every woman, every man is a star. Book of the law. This is a scientific explanation of the spiritual things we are believing. The book of the law says that chaos is needed for the birth of a dancing star. Chaos is melanin. Listen my people, here we go, this is the knowledge we should be receiving. I am about to go far. In every star burns a core and at that core is melanin. Once again at the core of every being is melanin that gives birth to a star. A star is a sun and the sun is the Christ. Christ is the soul and Christ is housed in the triple darkness of space, so as it goes called the night of the soul, melanin. The Christ is housed in a shadow and the shadow is melanin. As it is said, "Yea, Though I walk through the valley of the shadow of death I shall fear no evil." So the soul is the Christ, melanin is the substance that gives birth to the Christ. The sequel because when it is compacted together it makes an explosion into the Christ or star. The physical matter is an illusion, solidity is an illusion. The only thing that is real is the chaos or melanin which comprises of the seed or the atom or that particle of light called the child or magical child. Once the melanin is transformed it crystallizes birthing the term christos. And, christos is called the Christ. Christos, when it breaks through it comes with a shadow, that shadow is what you call the antichrist or shadow of God: that shadow is melanin, also called the Ayene in Hebrew meaning, nothing. So you have the Ayene, which is nothing or the triple blackness of space and then you have Christ or crystallized melanin. The yin and yang. The word Christomellows means black Christ, a word that was completely removed from the English language. In Greek it is called Chrisorios which is another form of the Christ. The yin or female passive forces is the melanin also called lamayen in the Egyptian Book of the Dead. The yang are the dominant active male forces of life. Comprised of the seed or the Atom that particle of light in which from the blood of (Iset) Auset, the triple darkness of space something began to illuminate and we have a miraculous conception from when consciousness said "let there be light" and the balance of that and darkness was because of love in which we create. Stolen and transformed from Iset the great mother and her son Osiris Horus and made a living cancer in us, is a European version in the form of a tampered with faith, Mary and Jesus Christ. That is a story of a people with melanin. Just as I explained the miraculous conception, scientifically there is an explanation for the resurrection. Amen Ra is associated with the sun; Amen meaning what is in darkness, hidden and what cannot be seen, Ra means what is visible, what is revealed, the revealed one. Out of the darkness forth comes the light. Melanin or pigment gave birth to our soul burning like an inferno of wisdom and innfinace crystallizing our cellular structure when the melanin comes together birthing the explosion and star, consciousness, the term cristos, or the word Christ is born. Light from our central sun or inner being penetrates while still in the physical form and flesh, we become what we are seeing which is forever, a higher level of consciousness, a new being, our senses levitate. The powers of melanin and its functions are simply miraculous and great. Black matter or Dark matter is a cosmic glue holding together a rapidly spinning galaxy and controlling the rate which the universe expands. This plasma in space, in the field at Quantum physics is made up of 25% Black Energy (stars) and 65% Black matter or Dark matter or as we say external DNA or Exoteric Mel-Anin (material). It is also a superconductor which can conduct electricity though still a mystery, we know that it can adapt to anything on this planet, it is original and organic. Melanin absorbs light, sound, and magnetism as well as convert light energy to sound energy or music; and back to light energy. To be put simply and plain, melanin gives humans the ability to be humane because it is the absorber of all frequencies of energies. As it comes in contact with sunlight we gain and receive new might, through music, radio waves, cosmic rays, it absorbs that energy, stores it, and passes it to other cells of the body so that they can charge and regenerate. It is tightly integrated into the nervous system. Pay attention and listen, its remarkable ability to accept and process energy and information in the form of light, sound, cosmic rays, and more make being black or melanin dominant akin to having a brain on the outside of one's body. Enabling a kind of hyper-perception. It is an extraordinary gift when considering how it enables us to interact with each other and the universe from every direction. Thoughts, feelings, and emotions are all emitted as forms of energy that are receivable and processable by melanin. Ancient Africans would hold conversations, send images and communicate via the drum from distances of thousands of miles away! They utilized their melanin and its ability to accept and process information in the form of energy waves. It is universal magic. Some may even call it "black magic", and that it is. Voodoo, sorcery, witchcraft, etc. All in which you are taught to be evil. Why? Because of the fears of a certain people who do not understand these powers. And because they fear for their existence, and do not understand, they label us as evil or of Satan. But here is the game I am playing. I will be that man, that prince of darkness, or bearer of light. That powerful, as stated earlier, christo-mellows. That black christ. This is a concept we should all take. That only chaos can give birth to a dancing star. Chaos is melanin in which the highest form resides in us. The world is ours to take. Something that white Amerikkka are fearful of, thus the reason why when many are in the presence of us, they are angered and become full of hate. Ancient Kemmitt was robbed by Europeans. and this ancient knowledge of inner illumination or inner powers and peace taught by Ethiopian and Egyptian priest became stolen and revised into secret sects. Sects like the Jesuit order, sects like Freemasonry and the Illuminati. This in which today only the most wealthy or rich are a part of. This is the knowledge of the Egyptian Mystery System, in which their schools taught universal knowledge...360 degrees. The Greeks and Romans, however, they could only master 32 degrees. Europeans lack our melanin and activation of their pineal gland to see things, by visualization, or through vision, mind power and of other realms to acquire the ability to master the cross, 360 degrees. We master magic while they try their hardest to create it. The Haitians used black magic to free themselves from the French. Melanin will eventually conquer the Earth and mankind. For it is the only thing that can stand up to the armor of the kings of the Earth. That is military power which was given to the Gentiles by the dark lord himself. Put 2 and 2 together and you will realize that the dark lord is us, a melanistic black people. Don't be afraid of the dark for the darkness is you and me. The triple darkness of space, 6 protons, 6 neutrons, and 6 electrons, thus the makeup of the carbon atom, whom we recognize as our father. The seed, magical child or the light. The Great I AM OR AMEN the hidden and Ra the revealer. Come together my melanistic people lets birth the star a burning soul revealing to those who desire light and true gold; wisdom, and knowledge. The resurrection is not too far. The time is now or never. So here we are.

You and Me...Me and You 2015

I wish that I could tell you that I am perfect. I wish that I could tell you that I am sane. The fact of the matter is that I am incomplete, and I feel worthless, because words just can't express how I truly feel, I'm yearning to show you that I am worth it and that is how I continue to maintain. The calm in your voice soothes me still, even though I am driven by it, nearly insane. You speak to me in music, a language so pure and so real, it brings life to this body, paralyzed by death when I'm not with you. My soul still moves, though, inside you, my soul still remains. That's love, your very nature. Don't hate me my Mahogany, my Heaven, just let me explain. You see the very existence that is us, man and woman is something that was always meant to be, we are the yin and yang. The truth about the light and darkness all of it centered around me and you, you and me. My dark nature, your flame. You are the material passive force of life, physical matter molded into existence by way of a special combination and mix, my energy. We are miraculous and something that they cannot explain. To me, it was as simple as 666, 6 protons,6 neutrons,6 electrons, the makeup of the carbon atom, the seed or light that magical child, the star or Christ as they called it. ADHAM the father and son are one in you and, through you because they are the same. To be separate from that, the organic is a detachment from GOD who is everyone and everyone is a combination of everything. We are material and energy, which is what is needed to create the children. We all are just as the stars born light in this universe. We are stars bearing light, separating into 3 parts. You then me, and then there is the core, the Earth's heart. Trust though that is us. We are the reason for love and lust. Your soul and your flesh which is me and you. To lust is to burn and burning is what stars do. It provides life and light and not just, so you could physically see, for inside us all burns an inner sun connecting everything and everyone, and everybody. Still though, that's just you and me. The term Christ is derived from the word Cristos, because of the crystallization of stars. When melanin is compacted together there is an explosion of light and life which is love and behold a star is born. Melanin, the cosmic glue of the universe holding and connecting everything together. When black and black come together miraculous happenings are dispersed. Dark matter and black energy merge as one entity. I now see how we are made to be infinite and forever, because you are my matter and I am your energy. I now see how we are the universe. Still though, that's just you and me, and me and you. We have been here since forever. And that I will put on anything. Anything other than the union between man and woman, would not be clever. Wherever there is this union there is life. Life is family. The word GOD comes from the Greek word GOT which means mother and father. They are the product of our living being. I speak these words to be truth. Truth is light, life and love everything between you and me, me and you.

The Marriage: To Get Your Body Off Into the Dark and Turn Your Soul On 2014

Today we give praise and worship and witness the union of GOD eternal for it is love and this phase its conquered quest in which the passions of the soul burns like a starry inferno glowing through the dark of flesh and when we recognize that love is life and life is blessed and there is no reason to turn back now. As GOD separated the waters into 3 sides you are the oceans, the sky is my pride or vice versa because I am bottomless when you stare deep into my eyes. My life is limitless when I stare into your imagination and that third side is at your mind's core which is my being here in this life, your life is my salvation. Even with this contemplation is something that most can't explain, how everything is maintained in perfect harmonic balance. The caption that it seems that nothing moves but us that is the trust that keeps us together under one name, one flesh, as is the sun and space it is amazing grace, the miraculous conception. For out of the darkness for comes the light, or the seed, the yin and the yang. Take my heart into your soul and let it beat with explosions then breathe the breath of life until we create future souls and give them our names and might, just as we did for God, and he did for us that night. This is the love and truth that I carried, it is the light, you are the night, this is the might of the marriage. TO GET YOUR BODY OFF Into The Dark and Turn Your Soul On.

ISrael ISet 2012

IS is for the Egyptian Goddess Isis, or Iset, Queen of the GODS and of Heaven, for her kingdom and powers are the epitome of what a black woman should be infinite, immaculate, and priceless but representative of what ISAT is, a queen of forever and eternity. Her name translates to "Queen of the Throne". Described by the Egyptians book of the dead as "She who gives birth to Heaven and Earth", was Queen in all 42 provinces of ancient Egypt, she owns. It is said that she knew the worth and power of the secret name RA, the king of the GODs, which gave her an incredible amount of power. Equal to her king in strength and characterized as the great enchantress, why she is reflected in her magic powers and in her knowledge in the arts of medicine and healing flourishes without flaw. She wears an empty throne upon her head, to me symbolizing her confidence in knowing that she is, and who is worthy to claim that seat, upon the throne of her mind, as she searches near and far for to find a deceased king. Who is one with and the son of Amen-RA, Osiris the morning star whose story became lost and cloned into the Roman Catholic Jesus Christ being. The biblical story meant to be interpreted literally was used as an instrument to control the minds and masses of the conquered Israelite people. Jesus Christ is the morning star, the sun. The 12 disciples are 12 of the 13 constellations, with thirteen being the Christ himself (In the Hebrew text some may reference, also, the 12 tribes of ISRAEL as well as the 12 disciples). Among the Roman Catholic church and Protestant denominations, Easter Sunday falls on the first Sunday after the first full moon after March 20th the nominal date of the spring equinox. Christianity's ancient linkage to sun and moon worship or obvious. The Sun completes its circuit of the Zodiac in a year. The year has 12 months, the Zodiac is divided into 12 houses representing the 12 divisions of the year. There are 12 cycles of the moon in a year. The Jewish calendar is a Lunar calendar, with 12 months following the 12 cycles of the moon.

A woman cycles twelve times in a year. The moon is the womb. The sun travels through the zodiac within that twelve month span. The sun representing the seed or light, consciousness or the head. This is a constant sexual play that has no definite beginning and no end. The microcosm and macrocosm are the same and operate in an identical way. The inner world or microcosm, everything from the skin within is the same as what is beyond the skin, and so you have sort of a perception of a heaven (being female) within a heaven and a God within a God (being male) concept thus it is said in the scriptures" greater is he that is in me than he that is in this world" or" so as it is in Heaven so shall it be on Earth". So the goal ultimately for us as black people is to create like our nature has ordained us to create because we are the natural creators of existence, thus creating our Heaven on Earth and send those who stand in the way of that straight to Hell like the Devils they are. This is us vibrating on higher frequencies, this is all science and to transform the state of reality within this physical realm we must transform the mind and vibrate on higher frequencies. To elaborate on my point about the inner world and outer world being rooted together as the Earth and planets revolve around the Sun, the macrocosm, the microcosm is the electrons revolving around the nucleus of the atom, mirrored in the same way, cycling the same way I'm not just saying we are God, science has proven that we are God. In the waters of Noone or the void (melanin) you have potentiality, potential energy where nothing moves, nothing exists. Usually there is going to be an event. In science it is known as the Big Bang. The Shabaka stone calls it betah, which is the conversion of energy at rest to energy in motion. This is known as the process of becoming or Kaperah as the ancients called it, when there is movement, nonstop creating the cosmos. In the beginning you have this potentiality that is acted upon from within. Look within, because it is what is within that will make you do something and convert your energy at rest and put your energy into motion. And, this happening in the ancient Egyptian stories is called the Atum (Ra) or Atom in science and Adam in the Christianity story. Atom is the thing that called all things into being, everything is on a frequency we all vibrate on a melanated frequency. We are all vibrations. The original vibration is the conversion of energy at rest into energy in motion or Betah or the atom, or wavelength. We are the vibrations of the original atom, or frequency, or wavelength. Truth recognizes itself. It is something that you can feel, and that is the original vibration, or frequency, saying 'Yeah, I'm here. I've always been here. (This is God or the atom, or frequency, or vibration).' We should all try to connect with the original frequency, or wavelength, so that we can be tuned in and process the information and history of the cosmos through the melanin. The creator or creation in the beginning was void without form or shape. The conception of the atom was a miraculous happening as something began to illuminate, move out of nothing. This is the conversion of energy at rest to energy in motion. The atom or Atum or Adam responsible for naming things into existence, did so by splitting in two. This is the Eve concept, and thus everything is done in a union or pair or the creation of that pair (our third dimension). And, this is where opposites come from, positive, negative, light darkness, man, woman. Thus, birthing all ancient deities in man and woman form. Everything has opposites, and these opposites are responsible for the elements of the universe on the periodic table. So, the union of man and woman creating is the natural flow of the universe. Everything is done in a union, so as you have the sun, the earth, and the moon. You have electrons, protons, and neutrons, father, mother, child, all cycling the same way, another union, so to speak, everything in threes.

This is why there is a holy trinity, it is all science. The number three is significant, because biblically, there are three heavens in which God resides in the third heaven. Scientifically and anciently, the cosmic waters of Noone or melanin, or the black liquid blood of Iset the goddess, were split into three parts, known scripturally as the oceans, the cosmos (or heavens), and the highest and most potent form of the melanin in man who is the seed, or the atom, or Atum. The light or consciousness. God is family, which is why it is so important for the black family to stay together. The universe depends on it. The occurrence that occurred was the big bang or the study of the origins of stars, superclusters, clusters, meteors, galaxies, solar systems, or organic life. In science, the thought or the atom is the origin of everything that comes out of the periodic table. Everything in the periodic table is a manipulation or addition to, or a subtraction of that one atom, which is the Hydrogen atom. Then there's Helium, then there's Lithium, number six is Carbon, etc. The creative force or thought or the atom wanted to know itself or thyself (knowledge of self), but could not because in the beginning it was pure energy. So within dark matter, and as it is said in the scriptures, the holy face of God was on the water. But, not H2O of today, but a cosmic black melanated liquid substance. A spiritual water or manifestation, which is the universe. The creator created a process our ancients called Kaparah or the process of becoming in which God will then know himself or herself in the physical form through this process of the creation and division of the atom. The creator knew it had to physically manifest itself by taking itself through a process. This process is the beginning of consciousness or life as we know it. As Dark Matter (melanin), being this movement in space in the beginning, and Dark Energy, which would be the inertia or repelling force(stars), come together to create consciousness and material, man and woman, or life . This constant movement and repelling of movement is the sexual nature of man and woman. After the experience of the evolution of the universe, then there will be an "inperiance" in which we would involve from within. He and she will come into existence from inside to out, again this is understanding the microcosm (inner world) which are the electrons revolving around the nucleus of the atom. And, the macrocosm (outer world) which is the planets revolving around the sun, or how we came to be a physical being. This is all just a study of the theory of relativity and quantum physics (the outer and inner world). Like, I stated earlier, everything is done in pairs or unions, this Universe is a perfect balance of a mixing of chemicals or (elements as on the periodic table). The mixing of one substance with another to create a more dominant substance. This is alchemy or black magic or sorcery, and I 'll bet this is the origin of the practice of all forms of medicine (eastern and western alike). The Universe is in perfect balance and has so to be to create something as miraculous as life, of this mixing of chemicals. I have Schizophrenia, which is an imbalance of chemicals in the brain, naturally for me, I am out order with the laws of the natural Universe (which would explain why some still say schizophrenia is demonic). I think differently from most. Some say I think backwards which may explain why I am so set on the creator and creation and where we come from because wiser men have said you can't know where you are going unless you know where you come from. This also explains why I chose to study and start at the back of the bible in the book of Revelations instead of the traditional. Traditions are a way to keep history repeating itself.

The New Testament and the story of Jesus is a story of a people with melanin describing astrological events with Jesus(the remodel of Osiris) represented as the morning star(revelations chpt.22:16) or the sun and the autumn and spring equinox and winter and summer solstice represents the positioning of the sun, or son. The birth, life, death and resurrection (the 4 sides of the cross). This is the celestial cross between the celestial equator, which is the spring and autumn equinox meeting the winter and summer solstice. This also represents the crossing of the sun traveling through all of the signs of the zodiac. The sun at the center, represents north, south, east, and west. The cross, which is really a mathematical, geographical, and scientific symbol has been made to have significant power spiritually. The bible (not to be taken literally) is a celestial metaphor and the stories within are allogores and full of celestial metaphores referring to the constellations, namely, us. Evidence of this is found all over the planet, from the positioning of historic landmarks to the way governments and religions are ran today. All over the world there seems to be a connection to this ancient system and we are the basis of all that we know today. They tell us that God doesn't want us worshiping the stars, but it is evident that sun and moon worship is essential and mirrors the lives of man and woman, because most of us don't know this is another reason why we are lost. Another plight by our enemies to bury and hide the truth deep inside of us just enough so we can't see our true power and possibly wake up and become one and use it against them. Began with black people, people. Remember where we all got life from. The black woman in which Egypt and the world still pay to this day hommage. There lying in the Sistine Chapel in Rome today where the Pope takes his place is an image of the black primadonna holding her infant son Horus, who she magically conceived, the re-incarnate of Osiris. This widespread image has been reinterpreted to refer to the Virgin Mary holding Jesus. Only the truth can feed us, if you hunger for more to be known, to spiritually survive we must realize that all of our knowledge of religion is derived from ancient Egypt and Ethiopia. This is the path we are on. ISet can also be credited with being the first deity known to man to introduce utopia, life after death. Her husband Osiris, who is also her brother is the ruler of the underworld and afterlife. I'll take this with my last breath, mothers, sistas love your man the black mack man has come to rule, but only if you rule him. For the word rule in Greek means Kingdom, for ISet the black woman is Queen of God, just as he is king of Heaven. Take this in remembrance of me forever, I am redeemed by the bloodshed, AMAN and ISET in Heaven. If this you feel, then rise ISRAEL. Bless them brethren.

IsRAel RA

We say AMEN after every prayer but how much do we know about the power and meaning of the name. Who is to blame for the black man's misfortune, Identity last, and lost in society. It surprises me that we have been confident this long. Despite the hundreds of millions of broken families, lives, and homes without clear cut evidence we still believe in that infinite, celestial power and that to reside with it is our right and that is where we belong. The name Amen or Aman means hidden. This is usually associated with RA's name. We must conclude that he was the personification of the hidden and unknown creative power which is associated with the primeval abyss, GODs in the creation of the universe and all that is in it. As a black man, I'm going to show you how high you should aim. The Am in AMEN means Ham and lord Ham. Ham means AM or AMEN. The name Adam was anciently spelled AdHam, Adamah, and Adamatu, meaning black or black blood and dark red Earth by the Hebrews and the Ethiopian-Babylonians, you and me. The Ad of Adam means father,

GOD or ELOHIM so you should believe as a black man that you are everything. In my mind there is a correlation between Adham and the Atom, Amen-Ra is also called Atom-Ra. The word or root, Amen, means what is hidden, what is not seen, and what cannot be seen, and the like. This proved by scores of examples which can be collected from texts of all periods. In hymns to Amen-Ra we read that he is hidden to his children and hidden to GODS and men. The name also hidden as well. His form or similitude also unknown to men. We should look within, why because that's where RA resides within, hidden to mortal eyes, and we are his prize living within him, I cannot pretend to be naive about the correlation of the Atom and Adham now I realize and believe that I am one with him. This is no coincidence from one Atom we have physical matter. Does it matter that the universe is black? It should, because that is what and where RA the truth is hidden in the darkness. Dark as my flesh I know that I am blessed when I say AMEN, For AMAN had the powers to construct the great pyramids and was a master in science, mathematics, astronomy, and agriculture. AMAN was king of the GODS royalty among other beings. AMAN was black and the black man will always be a king. Take this in remembrance of me forever I am redeemed by the bloodshed. AMAN and ISET in Heaven. If this you feel than rise ISRAEL and bless them brethren.

IsraEL EL

EL is for Elohim for in Hebrew it is referred to in the plural noun form meaning more than one. Stolen and revised identities, philosophies, and sciences have led us to believe in the Holy Trinity through the eyes of the Romans and Greeks, 3 male deities intertwined all into one. This originated from the Egyptian TRIAD, or ENNEAD whom consist of a Holy Father, and divine mother and child. We need to vibrate at a higher frequency level of consciousness so they can bring life back to the dead and truth to set us free so that our lives will be worth our while. The truth is ours to corral. From ISET, to Amen Ra, to Osiris-Horus. Holy father, divine mother and child. These are human like alien beings of a higher intelligence who created life through the scientific process on Earth, check the periodic table if you want to know how many different beings referring to the different resources, because of one atom. When asked about our origin from Chile to Cashmere from Italy to Easter Island, all of the myths answer, our species was created by Gods. The bible is formal, Elohim created man, Elohim is a masculine and feminine plural. It cannot be clearer, we were created by a highly intelligent people, whether we study the Greek mythology, the Assyrian encyclopedia, the epic of Gilgamesh, of Enki, of Cuchulain, the Vedas, the pyramids scriptures, the genesis according to Inuits, dogons or aboriginals, I found them unique and yet unanimous. Adorn with colors of their beautiful and precious colors, 600 traditions tells us the same story: that of Gods coming from the heavens to create a paradise on Earth, and shape men in their image. The ancient gods, our creators, look like us. We have 46 chromosomes and so do they, we are created in their image. They were giants among men, they were almighty, they knew everything, they were immortal. They were watching the stars through tubes and crystals with extreme advanced technology, so they were also known as the guardians or the watchmen. They traveled all over the galaxy with their flying machines and they visited planets and stars. They are often associated with the brightest star in our galaxy, Sirius (Iset) and the constellation Orion(Osiris) are the pleiades. In the book of revelations, the pleiades are the seven stars that the messiah (I won't say Jesus) holds in his right hand, which are the seven angels, that is the Atom or Adam, namely us. The former gods created short lived, intelligent being "ephemerals". They educated their creatures all they need for living, provided that the "ephemerals" worked hard in their mines and fields mining for gold. Gold was extremely important to the Anuki or Elohim. It is the greatest conductor of energy. They needed enough gold to rebuild the atmosphere on their home planet of Nibiru or planet X, which modern science recently discovered through high powered telescopes; but the ancients were able to see and know of and depicted them on the heiroglyphs (studied by archaeologist) who were unraveling Egypt (Kemmitt) thousands of years before. Nibiru swings into our orbit in the solar system every 26,000 years causing cataclysmic events not only to the earth but also to the other planets in our solar system. This is the easiest way for the Elohim to travel across the galaxy and get to the Earth. In the bible, the genesis tells that God created man, but the original version is this: Elohim created the Adam. Born out of the waters of noone or melanin the yin or female passive forces. Elohim is plural and Adam is a collected name. The bible should say the celestial androgenes created the humans; female humans because women were first made for the pleasure of the gods or the Atom (Iset to Osiris and Nephtys to Set.) Matriarchy was long the rule even after the onset of males who were also abused by the amazons, an elite troop of planetary matriarchy. The only trace of these facts that the bible maintains is the enigmatic first wife of Adam, Lilith. By herself, the semi-divine Lilith, summarizes a millenia of matriarchy on Earth. The males revolution has been through it. The brand-new patriarchate wanted to eradicate all traces of the domination of women, at the same time it also eradicated Rama, because his name, as his work reminded: hated matriarchs. Ra (Amen or Atom) the male original principle Ma (as in TahyaMAt or Iset) the female original principle. All the bible tales are described by ignorance or by calculation. The facts are distorted by countless interpretations over the centuries. We've got to overhaul, to label, or to resemble ancient mechanics. How can one imagine that the earthly paradise, the beautiful garden of eden was not of this world. It was in the world, but it belonged to another far far world: The pleiades. In fact, the garden of eden was a gigantic space ship (thus where the idea of the mothership originates) where the planet's developers, led by their leader King Anu (Anuki or Elohim) came to plant the Earth and boost human genetics in Northeast Africa. They manipulated the genes of plants to create grain, the genes of wild beast to create domestic species. Once the paradise was on Earth they went back to the stars. Before they managed to create us, our creators did many trials and a lot of mistakes starting with human- animals, details of which are bound in all mythologies. In Egypt, the pantheon has a wild variety of animal gods, besides Horus the falcon or Anubis the jackal; in Greek mythology, there are the centaurs with the body of a horse, the satyrs with goat's feet, the Minotaure of Crete, not to mention the gods who take animal forms; among the Dogons in West Africa. In the Mahabharata and other texts of ancient India, the very rich pantheon comprises numerous animal gods, such as Ganesha the elephant-man or Hanuman the ape-man. Are these hybrids metaphors or genetically engineered monsters. Our creators did other test with no result: the dwarfs, the giants and numerous human machines created for their service. We have kept them in memory under various names: Homo erectus, the yeti, Homo habilis the sasquatch, or Neanderthal. Then by a new genetics hocus pocus our designers transformed the primordial androgynous in man then in a woman, the story of the rib taken from Adam is true. Here is scientific truth. The XY chromosome pair has one "rib" in less comparing to the XX pair. This rib- or rather the missing side- is simply the segment which is missing from the Y to become an X. Thus were born Eve and Adam. By genetics. Yet for centuries we have understood literally this legend which was a disguised scientific explanation. So man and woman were created by flying androgynes. Gods and Goddesses descending from the stars. Genetics would have created the human species. But the human race already existed, since our creators were also human. It is not the creation of mankind that the story of Adam describes. It is a recreation, an improvement of the pre-existing species. If we compile the different mythologies, we can see that our creators did multiple experiments in genetics that often resulted in nonsense. Among all of these failed attempts, or unfulfilled species, ours wanted to survive, and here we are. Found everywhere is the trace of tragic genetics experiments tried by our creators. We are the special ones, out of all of Gods creations, because we have the pineal gland. This gland in our foreheads is the foundation of consciousness or light, namely we have a soul. Which is extremely important to our creators. The correct meaning of Elohim is "those who come from the sky." this is something of importance that we may have found, thanks to AMEN Ra the sky is dark like my flesh and flourishes from the moan of a woman which is life's prize and most precious and glorious sound. For that is the only way that we can have life, man and woman producing a child. 3 male deities intertwined are corrupted and such a union seems to be too foul. The Egyptian Ennead means nine, which reminds us of the 9 physical dimensions in all of creation where consciousness creates order with material (dark matter).The Ennead consist of 9 Gods and Goddess and are the 9 physical dimensions in all of creation .Starting with the sun or the seed, the light or the sperm-life of the solar system, which is the Atum-RA or the atom in science or Adam in Christianity. Remember, as I stated before, things are done in opposites are pairs, unions so to speak. So, you have the god Atum RA. Then there is the goddess Shu whom is space. Next you have the god Tefnut whom is the vibration or the cosmic water in space. Then there is the goddess Nut who is the atmosphere or what is between Earth and space Then there is the god Geb who the ancients viewed as the Earth. The next four are the star children of Atum who make up the cosmic life of the cosmos. Osiris whom is death and ruler of the Heavens and underworld is also associated with the sun or son. Then there is Iset whom is life and the mother of creation. She is melanin and we refer to her as Mother Nature. She is the beauty of life, that nurturing force .Osiris and Iset are married and are also brother and sister. Then there is their brother Set, who is also melanin and the male force or side of life. The word Satan comes from the Egyptian word Set and is associated with the planet Saturn (Capricorn's ruling planet) because Saturn is the 6th planet from the sun and the 6th most visible planet that we can see with the naked eye also called" the most high". Think about that, the 6th planet from the sun and the 6th most visible planet that we can see. Man is the sun. Every element on the periodic table is found in the Sun. The Sun can really be credited for the beginning of the known universe because every element that is on the periodic table is first found in the Sun and then in the known universe. The basic five elements needed for creation, nitrogen, helium, oxygen, hydrogen, and carbon are not only found in our Sun but also it is needed for the make up of space and the universe. More importantly than that, it is also the make up of the human being and melanin as we know it. The universe is made up of melanin, and there are two types of melanin. Pheo melanin is found in people with yellow to pale skin tones namely people of European, Arab, or Asian descent. Eu melanin, which is a black or brown substance, is the make- up of the universe and stars and is found in people of African descent, thus birthing the term hue-man. Knowing that the Sun, melanin, and human beings all have the same basic five elements tells us that the Atom or Atum(Amen)-RA or Adam is the Sun or Son, the name Adam means God or Elohim, this meaning man is the sun or source to all of creation. The worldwide image or symbol of the star is the 5-point image of what we conceive of what a star looks like. You have the head at the highest point of the image followed by the next two points which represents the shoulders and arms and finally, you have the last two points of the star image, the legs. This is not a coincidence. The 5 point star resembles the outstretched human body. Symbolized as mind over matter, the 5-point star is what is known as a pentagram, and is derived from the words pentacle or pinnacle, meaning at the highest point or perfection. This is all science and the great scientific minds of the world are revealing bits and pieces of the story. There is a whole lot that they aren't telling us though, and that is by design, there is a lot that they are hiding or that they don't want us to know, but with what we do know it is not hard to piece the puzzle together. The Egyptian goddess Iset is physical matter, melanin or space, Osiris also a star child of the Atum is also the Sun or Son as well as Set. Set is the chaos (melanin is chaos), destruction and sadness also the dominating and violent force of life. He is life in the male form also known to be associated with the sun or son; called the black sun or son by the ancients this referring to the blackness of space (melanin). Set was jealous of his brother Osiris and wanted to be the ruler of the kingdom of the Heavens which meant being married to Iset. Being that they are both life the male and female form, this would only make sense. But Death, which is Osiris, was in the way, married to the life. So Set murdered and mutilated his brother and scattered his body into 13 pieces which are seen as the 13 astrological signs and constellations. This is why Osiris is seen as death and why he is associated with the underworld. He was meant to be sacrificed and   reborn as Osiris-Horus, his son, who was magically conceived by Iset after putting Osiris's body back together. This again is the miraculous conception. The last of the star children is the wife of Set and Iset's twin sister, Nephtys. She is what is between life and death. Thus, placing herself in a very formidable position in all of this. She is the place where this all happens at the center of all of this happening. The ancients believed that there were worlds within worlds or universes within universes and so on. They believed that we are the micro-life of the solar system or we are inside of another being so to speak. They believed that our solar system was an actual living being; thus they viewed these gods as actual people .We too have micro-life within us and thus becoming worlds or universes in our own selves to the micro-life within us. The ancients viewed the Sun the Earth and the Moon and stars as actual living people, and that train of thought may not be far-fetched, giving what we know about the microcosm and macrocosm (The inner world and outer world). We too, are places just as the sun, earth, and moon to this micro-life within us. This mixing of gods and goddesses are the same as the mixing of chemicals which create the elements (as on the periodic table) which create the creation. This again is Alchemy, or the study of melanin also called sorcery or black magic. This is scientific and spiritual, and the proof and realization of this truth can heal us all as individuals. Indivisible, the active and passive forces at the deepest level of reality called the Absolute, where all is one, before any differentiation, the 2 forces meet and are truly one. We live this miracle. In the beginning there was the word, and the word was God and the word was with God (father, son, holy spirit or mother;) the ability to say, "I am". This state is often referred to as the void, as it has no form and no movement, just perfect balance. All of creation is contained within this void in a dormant state, overjoyed because life is harmonic caption. From the absolute the first differentiation between the active forces (male side of creation), the yang and passive forces (the female side of creation), the yin come together creating consciousness and material. From these two differentiations of the absolute (or God) everything is created and spiritual. Consciousness molds material into form and incarnates into this form. It is a constant sexual play where the female material substance or matter yearns to be molded by the male conscious and the male yearns to enter the female and mold her substance into form. This is the way our nature behaves, how our life is born. There was no beginning there is no end. Creation is and has been a constant sexual play. When formed, God is the union of the active male conscious(energy), and passive material substance of the female (or matter). That truth cannot be changed and has sustained and is here to stay even in the after. We have the ability to say "I am" as in the Great I Am, the conscious the male side of life. The AM in the word Adham means lord or Elohim it also means Ham which means black. This universe also known as the Heaven is black and is to our father Adham, his wife and what we call life. We say Amen after every prayer. Amen Ra is also called ATOM Ra, from the Atom we have physical matter or creation, the female passive force in which we call mother nature. A family united is the reason why evil will hate you. When I think of the ancient Romans and Greeks and the leaders of their empires, believers in their homosexual behavior make me think and want to speak on the subject of what has happened to the Roman Catholic Christian Church. A demon of homosexuality is living within as God and made mainstream in this world. That's why this world will be set on fire. To deny the truth of creation stemming from the man and woman union and presence, is blasphemy to God who is that combination and us, realizing that is the essence. For blasphemy is the cursing of the Holy Spirit. Denying the very thing that gave us life, the powers of the woman incarnated from Egyptian Goddess ISET, the mother of GOD, thus becoming the comforter, that is the nature of a woman not a man, I know you hear it. Holy for the father and spirit for the son, that is our true trinity and how they are one. ISET, the mother, Amen Ra, the father, Osiris Horus, whose Egyptian truth gave birth to the story of Jesus, the son (sun). There is a lot of ancient Egyptian mystery in Hebrew history. The Greeks and Romans stole philosophy and scientific technology from black people when they conquered Israel in 70 A.D. Then set in place a 2500-year plan that would bring about the destruction and division of our once powerful, in which we put the Hue in the word human race and formidable united family; through the construction of a religion who created a GOD formed of foul and lustful desires, evil oppressive intentions and corrupt understanding. All so that we would fall far from our original grace. Since creation was built from consciousness the way to destroy the creation would be to start with the conscious and that has happened. They destroyed the male side of life by making us submissive and passive to their religion and lustful desires, those are feminine traits. This first took place in the early church when texts were being translated into their language. Then they infiltrated the ancient religion and Paganism was introduced to the text. Roman Emperors who came and went, became corrupted by new power oversexed with the control of a cursed people. Homosexuality flourished and the flame lit in the church could not be extinguished. The GOD as we once knew it, our conscious, was being transformed from a dominant active male presence into a submissive passive feminine state of being who has seen this. Being that the originality of the church is based off of the creation story this entailing the creation of family through the Egyptian Triad or Ennead or the Holy Trinity. It is to my understanding that they destroyed us by destroying GOD in us first, our Glory, through the division of the family. Thus, those who want to destroy GOD have figured this out. They don't want us to know who GOD is and the truth to the story so if they destroy our conscious (the male side) then there will be no material, no matter, life could not exist because the woman would be irrelevant. Remember who you are brothas and sistas we are created in their image forever together we are meant. We are brothers and sisters because we have a mother and father in nature and those two sides are evidence. Elohim or Ham in Hebrew is referred to the plural meaning more than one. Aman, ISET, and Osiris are one, the Elohim just as we are one with the Atom. our father who art in Heaven, who we see when look up into the eve, take this in remembrance of me forever I am redeemed by the bloodshed AMAN and ISET in Heaven, if this you feel then rise ISRAEL and bless them brethren. Denial is one of our enemies, may our enemies decease now that we have a sense of truth, may our conscious be at PEACE, forever.

I Hope You Understand
(non- rhyming piece) 2017

I have paranoid schizophrenia. It is a very tragic disease and a lot of the time I am out of touch with reality. I call it tragic because I have no, or little feeling left inside. My soul has been tormented by the audio and visual hallucinations that is associated with this disease. I hear 7 voices who are family members on one end of my mind, and then an 8th in the form of beautiful female entity, her name is Heaven. The 7 voices used to be in competition with the 8th (or Heaven) over who I was more loyal to. I am 39 now, this went on for 15 years or more. The 7 beings new that I was crazy over Heaven. I fell in love with her in pre-school at the age of 3 years old. I can still remember the day I first seen her. I was mesmerized and possessed. To the point to where I was in a fight with a family member over who got a chance to sit by her at lunch time in pre-k. My family knew that this meeting between Heaven and I could be potentially dangerous to my psyche. So over the years I slowly forgot about her until I started seeking the kingdom. As the bible says, "seek the kingdom and you shall find." I began to wonder about life and my origins and her. So I educated myself on the history of men and gods and what is in this book is what I found. It was when I read the book of revelations when I first heard the voices. The voices were trying to convince me that, I as a man, was God. My reward for the acceptance of this train of thought, would be Heaven. I don't know when schizophrenia first appeared all I know is that I was depressed and suicidal my first year in college. I felt as if I was to intelligent to be here. I could see through the bullshit and frankly, I was tired of it. I was 18 then. That next year I came home from college and I moved in with my grandparents, the creators of those 7 voices. Their children are the 7 voices that I hear and dominate my thoughts. But equally as powerful was the soothing, relaxing comforting voice of Heaven, the eighth. Because of my fascination with Heaven, the seven voices had different test in certain situations for me to go through to determine whether or not if I was ready to receive her as she was to be granted to me. Physically I did not know where Heaven was but I was communicating with her with my mind or through telepathy. The voices were trying to convince me that I was the messiah, all of this seemed too good to be true. But before anybody else can believe it I had to believe it first. Remember I was going to kill myself, until I started hearing the voices. At first Heaven and the voices were battling over who would have control over me. Then because all of this happening to me I became angry more angered at the fact that whoever God is or was, he was playing way too rough with me. I felt like God was playing a very dangerous mind game with me. This made me bitter and so angered to the point to where I was challenging God. I didn't care about my salvation. I was already in Hell so God could not threaten me with flames or torment. I was already tormented. If it wasn't for my mother who was there with me every step of the way, I would have ended this life. I became full of hate. I didn't care anymore about the future of my people. I was turning my back. All I know is that I tried my best with the tools that I was given to bring to my people this message of redemption and resurrection. But the level of ignorance was at its peak and I grew exhausted trying to free those minds who were held in the chains and shackles of man-made religion and tradition. This was interfering with my thought-process. I felt like my mind was being played with. The hallucinations were driving me insane. More so I felt as if God was teasing me with heaven. It got so bad to where I could not go to church and bear to hear any mentioning of the word Heaven. I just wanted to die. I could not fully believe that I was the savior until I found her first, to see if my thoughts of what Heaven should be were true. I even abstained from sex from 18 to 24 in hopes of impressing the 7 voices, so they would grant me with Heaven. The 7 voices are the equivalent to the 7 spirits of god, the 7 nations, the 7 stars of the pleadies, the 7 seas and the 7 angels, 7 letters also spell the word Heavens. I knew deep down in my heart I had to find her before I ran out of time. I became angry at the spirits and at Heaven to the point to where I did not want to live anymore. Then instead of bickering over who I would serve, the 7 and Heaven joined together to entice me to want to keep living. I always believed in a messiah, but I never imagined that it was me. A vast majority of europeans are out to destroy any hint of a black messiah and are jumping through hoops to make sure that one never appears. I saw this revelation as justice finally granted to a people who have suffered much massacre and torment because of skin color over the centuries. This was redemption for my race. That this world will cycle back into the power that was stolen from us and hidden throughout the Roman empire. I eventually found Heaven and developed a deep friendship and relationship. I explained to her what the voices were trying to show me, ironically, she was a psychiatry major and that she had an interest in people who have schizophrenia, was this a coincidence are was this destiny. She began to council me. My talks with her were reassuring. I was screaming for help and she was helping me. However my mother and my doctor were against me having a relationship with her. They did not think that I should listen to her or that she should be counseling me, because she was not qualified or professionally trained to deal with a schizophrenic. She was everything I prayed for sweet, religious, spiritual, witty and beautiful. I told her that this world belonged to us and we have to seize it back. She agreed but she did not want to relinquish that christian idealism and mysticism. She was loyal to Jesus and what made me the Anti-Christ was that I was trying to knock that christian slave mentality out of her system by providing her with documented facts that proved me to be for real. Jesus or Jezeus (roman catholic zeus) never existed as a physical person. I can say that I AM. Jesus became my enemy. The more she praised Jesus the more angry I got. How can I believe that I am king if my potential mate sees the symbol of white supremacy, Jesus, as her king?   Revelations chapter 19 talks about the bride of Jesus being the kingdom of heaven. Like I said before, Zeus never existed as physical person, I can say that I am. My goal was to set up the kingdom of Heaven on Earth. First I had to prepare Heaven and Earth. The Earth being my beloved Mahogany, the mother of my children whom I met during my search for Heaven. I had to show her that I was for real when I told her Heaven was with me. I had to prepare them for the transition by educating them with truth. Heaven and I are both Leos(lions) a king and queen, we are both dominant by nature and we always have to be the light or life of the party. Our ruling planet is the Sun and we are both fire signs. Mahogany is an Aries, and is a fire sign as well and her ruling planet is Mars, and red and gold are my favorite colors. In my left palm I have Heavens initials HP embedded in my hand, inside the H is the letter L. My father's name is Luther and he was born on the thirteenth of January, Heavens birthday falls on the thirteenth of August. 13 +13 is 26, thus I was born on the 26th of July. There are too many coincidences in this happening linking me and Heaven together. Now my doctor told me that she (my doctor) would destroy the voices and I told her that she could not because they are a part of me. She said "watch me". All I know is that my family members started to die off one by one physically. This sunk me deeper in the abyss. I was depressed and angry that the sources of my power or gift began to die off. I was on some heavy mind drugs that was prescribed by my doctor that had me in a zombie state. It got to the point to where I began cursing Heaven and those 7 spirits. I was heartbroken because it seemed as if I was the only one who could see the future, everyone else was blinded by society. It made me fill as if I was all alone in my thinking. I did not give up though, I eventually traveled through Heaven and I realized that the only thing that can hurt me was her lack of knowledge and   her ignorance. Which was showcased when I told her that I have been married to her spiritually this whole time since the beginning of time. I told her that I was her husband. That struck a nerve; because she went left, she went off on me. Maybe because I was already common law married to Mahogany, the Earth. Knowing that most of the caucazoid race or caucasion will attempt to destroy any hint of a black messiah, I had to remain faithful that god did not bring me this far in my thinking for nothing. How can I save the world when I can't seem to save the spirits in Heaven? I sunk deeper in the depression. Schyzophrenia was formally known as demonic possession, but now we know that it is a chemical imbalance in the brain. The medication I take helps to correct this imbalance. But I have to admit I struggle to take it right. There are so many side effects that comes with the consumption of the medication. When I do not take it I find that I am very excitable and anxious. Sometimes I am up for more than 24 hours. I can't drift off to sleep to save my life. I am constantly pounded with visions or voices that want allow me to rest until I understand why this is happening. My soul has been drug through the mud. What's worse is that I can't pull this off by myself. I need the Heaven and the Earth to get behind me and have my back. Look, I come from the generation that produced black on black violence, promoted by the Gangster rap industry. Where you could get killed over tennis shoes or over a jacket or a nice car. Everybody wanted to be a gangster, be blood or crip. I, in my ignorance, could have gotten killed, or lost my freedom trying to be a gangster, then what would have become of my life, I would have never remembered Heaven and I probably would not have connected or met Mahogany, the Earth. So just take a minute to see what I am up against. My own kind who still believe in a fairytale, brainwashed so by religion to the point of being enslaved psychologically and eventually enslaved physically, again. Why are their more prisons and concentration camps being built than schools and universities? Who are they going to put in these prisons and camps? Black people. It is set up for us to fail if we are not careful. They kill us and get off scott-free. They wonder why we are so angry. Probably due to the some 2500 years of mistreatment and torture of the black race. The most evil form of racism was suffered by the black race from white AmeriKKKa. They want to cause an uproar in the black community, so they can introduce martial law and bring the military into play, to muscle anyone that they feel is a legitimate threat to their existence into the prisons and concentration camps. Ever heard of the King Alfred Plan? This was designed in the 1960's by the government because the earth was being vastly populated and they needed to come up with ways to maintain population control. They poison the drinking water, and foods that we eat. They kill us over here in this country whenever they feel the need to with various hate crimes and police brutality. They introduced genocide to some of the African countries, killing of the crops so starvation would take place. Then they can play on our psyche by showing images of starving sick black children then taking the donations and money for their own personal gain. The children never see or benefit from the money. They have robbed Africa blind of its natural resources, knowledge and history. All they give the people of Africa is man- made diseases and a bible. They put fluoride in our toothpaste which is a direct deterrent to the Pineal gland. They spray chem-trails in the sky in hopes to calcify our pineal gland, so that we cannot tap into our melanistic powers. They teach us in the churches that worshipping the sun and moon is forbidden by God, in all the while they knew that this references and mirrors man and woman. They are doing all of this because they don't want us to unite and take this world back. There are 7 billion people on the planet, 85% of those people are black or melanin dominated. We are the majority not the minority. I have the burden of trying to wake a spiritually dead nation with these truths. It's no wonder why my mindstate is fucked up. We all should have schizophrenia because of the psychological and physical trauma we have suffered. We still suffer from things that happened centuries ago because of documents like the Willie Lynch letter to the King Alfred plan. Still though this is something that my Heavenly father wants me to do, and even though it seems impossible, I still believe that it is possible. The universe is full of possibilities. I mean, this journey that I have taken has nearly destroyed me. I have done things out of my character just to bring my mind peace. Things that I am not proud of. I will confess that I have hustled people out of $20.00 here $30.00 there to feed my addiction to marijuana because that is the only way for me to have peace. To make matters worse I discovered that schizophrenia can spin Lupus and vice versa. I have Lupus Nephritas which we first discovered in 2007 when it attacked my kidneys violently. Because my kidneys were damaged so, I had to go through chemo treatments to boost my kidneys back to proper function. They used an extensive amount of steroids to shock my kidneys back into function. It is because of this that caused me to develop avascular nacrosis, or the deterioration of the bone in the hips. When the seasons change, I am so much pain that I am almost in tears. Mahogany often has to help me put on clothes or help me to the bathroom at night. She has taken good care of me. She is my foundation. Her love for me is what is holding me up as I take this stand. At least I know she still loves me unconditionally. I wish I could say the same for Heaven. There are no other women in my life, I never needed a lot of women. Just my Mahogany Earth and my Heaven was all I ever needed or wanted. The book of revelations talks about the messiah, being faithful and true to Heaven and Earth and that I have been. Since I started this test of faith some 20 years ago. The only women that I have been with still since I was 18 is Mahogany and Heaven. The reason for my celibacy for that period of time in my life was because well I don't like using protection I think it takes away from the feeling. So, to protect myself from aids and to show that I wasn't looking at Heaven with a lustful eye, I abstained from sex until I met Mahogany. I just could not wait any longer. Six years is a long time for a man, especially for a young man in his sexual prime. I had to be very strong to get through it. I was tempted many times but I had to be strong to prove myself worthy to be Heaven's king and the Mahogany Messiah. Heaven and Earth is all I ever wanted .That was all I ever needed. Heaven with her knowledge and spiritual wisdom, and Mahogany with her sweet personality, and loving nature. Both of them are beautiful worlds to me and words cannot describe how I truly feel for them. I was diagnosed with avascular nacrosis, which is the deterioration of the bone in the hip, in 2012, the same year that I shared that memorable experience with Heaven. I am currently taking opioids for the pain, but I can only get a few at a time because of their addictive nature. Also, I smoke marijuana as a substitute for the opioids and to help cope with the voices and visions. My addiction to marijuana has grown stronger because of this pain. I have sunk to the lowest of lows just to feed my addiction. I have pawned my daughter's electronic devices, sold Mahogany's deceased mother's belongings, some of which were antiques and had value. I sold it all just to feed my addiction. This is the darkest time of my life. It's like I don't have feelings anymore. My soul has become num. I mean physically I am here, but I feel a sort of a detachment or a disconnect from everyone and everything Lord knows I love my kids, but I feel a detachment from my immediate and extended family. I feel detached from God. My kids are supposed to bring me joy, I asked God many times why I can't connect with them. I try to pray about it, but the voices are so loud inside my mind that I have trouble concentrating on my prayer. So, I just stop praying. I don't get the joy I deserve when I play with my kids. Feelings are forced, forced laughter, nothing natural anymore. It is frustrating and a lot of times I verbally attack them because of my situation and I know that's wrong. I am disabled so I cannot work. This makes me feel less than a man not being able to work and provide for my family and be the breadwinner. Now I have the whole world on my plate, but the question is am I still hungry enough to digest it all. With this book, I hope to eat. This piece was for anyone who may not understand why I do some of the things that I do as a schyzophrenic. Most people who have this condition are very intelligent and or even highly intelligent. Some are just able to express their thoughts and feelings better than others., which could be the ultimate determiner of how an individual turns out, is a productive citizen are not. I myself often have evil thoughts of doing harm to not only to myself but to others. I often have thoughts of killing people who do me injustice or out of frustration I may snap and have this fuck everybody attitude, where I just shut down and want to destroy the nearest thing around me. The whole reason why I am here to have peace, but I see do to the beast like nature of society, that is going to be easier said to attain than done. We have the ability to connect with and vibrate on higher frequencies and become sentient, celestial beings and curb that beast like nature that we all possess due to the creation process in which our creators took from all four parts of the animal kingdom to create us. The reptilian brain, mammalian brain, neo cortex, or our rational brain, and then there is the frontal lobe. This is where the pineal gland is located. The pineal gland is the gateway to inner and outer dimensional power in which we become multi-dimensional and our bodies are illuminated, full of light ; This is what the third eye represents or the all seeing eye of Osiris .This gives us the ability to see life from a universal perspective and rise above our beast like nature and vibrate on a higher frequency or realm of consciousness . We as a people have yet to arrive at this point. Our beast like nature which consist of us thinking eat first for survival fight for territory and survival, mate for survival is where the concept of evil and lust comes from and thus gives birth to the satan concept; our inner dimensional selves illuminate our bodies to the point to where we have no need for those worldly desires. The problem is there is a select group of people who want to keep us from tapping into that power. They construct deterring tactics to make sure that man stays enslaved by religion and the media and politics so that we are constantly afraid and dependent on them. What's going on in society is what has driven me insane. People are so insensitive to the next man, and frankly, I am beginning to not like people very much. As for the church the churches should form a union and function as corporations do. Its sole purpose would be to educate the congregations with this knowledge. Its curriculum should be to educate with truth not a lie in the form of Jesus. It should also be economically and politically driven. Their focus should be on what's happening in the black community and poverty-stricken neighborhoods, at the head of this union the church should have a board of directors and a council that they are to report to. I think the wealthiest churches should have a league or team of high powered high-priced lawyers funded by the churches to help bring justice to situations of injustice that we see time and time again in society and in the black community. These lawyers should be the best in their profession and should serve the people at no charge because they are compensated by the churches. The truth is out there, we need the church to stop with the lies and allogores and deliver the truth to the congregations. There is a psychological war happening right before our eyes and if we don't wake up and stay woke, we are all going to die. My mother and my uncle G, two of the voices that I hear, inspired me to write this book, and once said to me" The truth will set you free." That goes for all of those enslaved and brainwashed christians and muslims alike. Only the truth about who we are will set us free. The churches should produce funding for more schools and universities to be built teaching the value of this knowledge that was stolen from us. For the larger churches, tithes paid by the congregations should allow churches to have after school programs and activities for kids who have working parents. This should help in further educating the youth with the truth, and keep our kids active and off the streets and at the hands of the enemy who are killing our youth. As for what I go through, I am so paranoid. I often think people are plotting on me, trying to set me up. Sometimes I believe that the government has tapped into my mind and can control and hear my thoughts as ridiculous as that sounds, sometimes I feel people know what I am thinking or I know what they are thinking. I have visual hallucinations. Sometimes, everything will turn gold all around me and this would last for about a minute. It is the scariest thing when I consider what the voices have been telling me. I feel like God has something against me, it's like he is pissed because I found Heaven not once, but twice because I met her when I was 3. If you believe Jesus (jeZEUS) is God then you should understand why I feel like that spirit, which is the true devil, wants me dead. Roman emperor Constantine was a Zeus worshipper it was he who formed the council of nicea and ordained the Christian bible close to 400 years after the invasion of black Israel in 70 a.d. and Israel fell under Roman rule. Years later he rose to power and he created this council and this the beginning of the Roman Catholic reign and era, with white Jesus(Zeus) becoming the symbol of white supremacy at a time when the trans-atlantic slave trade was in its infancy. The letter J did not exist in any language until about 500 years ago around the time European settlers forbade Africans to learn how to read and tried to make slaves of the native black people who were already in the Americas. The natives would just run away and escape to freedom because they knew the land. When they failed to make slaves of the natives then they went to Africa to transport slaves who were not native to the land. Therefore, if they escaped they would be easily found because they did not know the land. Zeus has never existed as a man and the name Zeus dose not translate into the word savior in any language, so how could he be God. This is why I feel like Jesus is against me not only because of what I plan to do with Heaven, but also because I want to unite my people, and give them this world back which means we have to promote the truth which leads to black supremacy in many ways , not to say that as a race that we are better; but the truth of the matter is that we are the origin, the original species . Everywhere archaeologist dig they find evidence of the black race. Now are we alien? Well, we might very well be. The bible does say that we are just passing through (life on this planet). Am I crazy for being able to see and formulate this perspective this way, are am I just outside the reality. To be honest, I feel like both. The kingdom of Heaven is knowledge and wisdom, it is golden light and life, just as the Sun(Son). It is something everyone can attain, but we have to believe that we are all one, one body that makes up the physical universe. What you do to your fellow man ultimately affects the world and everyone in the world, it is the law of attraction; the energy you put out (whether be positive or negative) is what will come back to you. The bible says," He who leads into captivity(slavery) shall go into captivity". We have been enslaved for too long, all of us black, white, red, brown, and yellow, from one end of the Earth to the next, everyone is being programed to be a slave through religion, media and society as a whole, whether mentally or physically. There is a select group of extremely wealthy people who want to control and dominate the world. It is not about black and white anymore, but rather" the haves and the have nots". I refuse to be a slave anymore and you should too, it is time to unite and become the masters of our own destiny. This is the truth about me and you and what I am dealing with, I hope you understand.

The Return of the Dark People Vol. 1: The Intro 2012

You probably believe in heroes those of whom are men and women of renown whom defeat their foes and bless those in need of salvation and inspire generation after generation from then when they achieved their victory, till now. If so, then let me explain the powers and intelligence of a race of beings being the most extraordinary thing to happen in an infinite possibility of happenings. For the reason and relevance of this piece is to reveal to all who are in the dark the greatest spark known to mankind. To bring the power of peace to all human beings leaving every one of them satisfied and confident because they recognize their abilities and have been taught and mentored how to use them for their own benefit and to benefit of others, they were created for the lovers of the heartbeat and the rhyme. You know they are coming when you hear the music and the beat. A rhythmic race of beings who can sense and feel and give any and every vibration of the mind and inner most parts of the self and manipulate them to their frequency which is something other than this Earthly physicality, and things of this kind, who without the abilities of the dark people, would not even exist itself. They are physical matter birthed from one atom in which they call father. He is the reason for creation, from every physical terrestrial plane to every spiritual celestial plane. They have created the cosmos and the galaxies for their pleasure, and have embodied themselves inside of them, forgetting their abilities. They have become carnal and vain extending their creative and immaculate powers to their vessels giving light to brand new imaginations. New creations as was in and embodied structure as their creators. They are the same. From galaxies, to planets, to human people these are the barriers we must break if we are to see a sequel to see if the dark people can bring back stability to an unstable violent mind, a violent world and universe for they are all one with each being in the dark. The dark flesh and the dark universe are one in the same. The conscious is the universal plane. Everything inside are the powers and abilities of the dark people. A spiritual thought manifested into the physical and because it was out of balance when it happened, because more admiration was for the physical creation instead of the spiritual creator, we now have good and evil. The rhythm of creation of every thought to every being is the bridge and balance, so here is the beginning of the quest, to show how and why we are blessed and help return the forgotten powers and gifts back to the dark people.

The Return of the Dark People Vol. 2: "The Father Atom"

He is the basic building block of life as we know it. He is confident and strong in his abilities to create poets of anything and everything he desires, the higher form of mankind himself, a spark in a darkened vessel, who knows that his spark burned, and darkened this vessel until it hardened dispersed and became cold. So cold that this undeniable truth became lost in today's youth. They don't accept this thought as real. This is proof of ignorance and it shows it. But if there is a way to that celestial and infinite thought in which the energy in Atom said "Let there be.", and there was, whether be light or darkness if there is a way back to that infinite energy only our Atom knows it. Back to a place in which there are no physicalities, just spiritual energies and realities of powers of a celestial mind in which is at the center of anything that is. That is to say, can you fathom a place beyond our darkened cold universe? In this next verse, I will speak of a people who can. The Dark People.

By decoating their Atom is the key back to that celestial place let's start by amazing the grace that is solely laced inside of me.

The Return of the Dark People Vol. 3: "The Powers of the Dark"

The darkness hides things. Sometimes objects, things your mind projects, other beings, so that if you choose to enter the darkness blindly without the proper essentials, what you have left exposed is I suppose like bleeding meat dangling to a hungry uncaged lion, your mental. Psyche has no power when it comes to reality. You can believe, in fact with all your might, that's essential, but the fact of the matter is that in actuality what you don't see or tend to overlook can hurt you if you run right into it. That's when your life flashes before your eyes and you remember. Stop you dead in your tracks the power of the Dark has an impact of just that. Be careful when you approach me. Proceed slow when you decide to move close to it. You never know what could be lurking there just waiting on you to run into it. Thus as it goes for those who oppose the DARK, they are all fascinated with them, with us. Always exploring the mind and physical attributes of our being but not without being direct with us about what they claim they've discovered, uncovered and are seeing. Got us all believing that they created this, that all of these powers came from them when in reality they wouldn't even exist if it weren't for the Dark People, because they were created by them. The Dark People are physical matter itself. Whose father, Atom is embodied inside of their creation. His energy is fueled by their admiration of themselves, because that's him and only through him can they change the situation. And change it they will, however that may come to be. The Dark People possess powers beyond the wildest imagination, could you imagine a different type of scenery, I mean, something other than what you or me can physically see, a different type of matter other than this physicality. They possess the type of power that most would consider to be absolute, able to create lives and take lives all in one breath. Still showing their might, they will dare anything in life to test. They rest in the confidence that they are right, that they are life and the fact that we exist is proof of their truth. They created the cosmos for their pleasure, everything to operate in a rhythmic harmony. Proceeding to the beat of their heart was the song of creation. Life's treasure. Music in the form of Galactic art. This song continues to form us as human beings. They embodied themselves in the form of galaxies, stars, constellations and planets. Eventually, they created and embodied themselves inside a humanoid being and said, Amen, after they seen him understanding the universe's plan to expand it. They multiplied thus becoming man intertwined, the rhyme to that creation song, and the only way for the Dark People to return to that spiritual scene, celestial, non-physical state in which atom resides. The spirituals here in this realm call it home. Even though the way back to the throne is to provide the DNA and decode the Atom of the Dark People, to them that is something not known. You see though they are masterful creators, there are these creations which ultimately causes their downfall. In love with these creations, it was the beauty that entrapped them and caused them to forget their immaculate powers which in turn became one with the creation and not now with the creator which is why it is now up to us to bring their kingdom, it is now the hour. They are with us now, right now as I speak these words. The plight and trap against their enemies has been set and energized by them and what you heard. You see they can sense every vibe of their mind and innermost parts of the self. They have gotten us to realize the way back home by manipulating our vibes to their frequency. They have shown us to look inside ourselves. But, beware there is an enemy. Those who denounce the Dark People's authority and abilities, want to bring oppression to those who are dark. It is up to us, our father Atom can be of no help.

The Return of the Dark People Vol. 4: "Collective Amnesia"

Now the children of Atom, Chrono, Mat, En, and Space, made up all of the physical kingdom of Atom. even though the creators were celestial, the physical kingdom itself is an illusion; created to bring a sense of place and wealth to the children. The best in them was their health and grace and that is why the decision was made to commence fusion. And so there was EN the eldest and short for "energy" the first to be released. Then there was MAT, short for "matter" nothing can make sense of her …. The second to be dispersed into what she called nothing her little sister, Space. Space was decorated and infinite in all directions like her father's kingdom, her mother, the Illumini, peace. But violent, dark and cold in her abilities to entrap mass. If there was a resurrection back into the celestial past, to say the least, it would travel through her, and only through her can it not decease. Then there is Chronos, a translation of time. Like his sister, he is infinite and decorated with happenings in this universe here, his story will remind us all of how we got back to that nonphysical state, in the upper-tier, his story will remind us all of how we got to man and mankind. So, they are matter, energy, space, and time. Known as the MEST, they are the best at what they do, creating physical entities and life forms until life evolved into physical mind, man, me and you. But here is the dark truth, once man was created, there was nothing left for them to do. They embodied themselves inside so until their illusion began speaking truth exploding through the laws of physics with our love for life being the proof, we live it, sometimes with the very passion, that the Illumini (the light) has for her children. We consider our lives to be the same, man and woman, only doubt can separate the powers within that we're given. The Illumini began to doubt that her children would not find their way back into the spiritual. The Dark People as a result began to forget their immaculate nature and became lost inside the physical. Not until worlds saw the likes of dark human flesh was there birthed a way back into the future, like their predecessors before them, they were a miracle. The Dark Man was the re-incarnate of the Dark People. So to the point that the first human created was named Adham to be the representative of the celestial mother and father Illumini and Atom and possess a hue in the burnt likeness of his children the Dark People. Thus we have human people. From the morning star Adham we have everything. His bride taken from him made to be the harborer of life, the wife called Eve and by way when we see into the night we can see our true infinite life and what we are really meant to be. Adham and Eve produce children of two dark complexions they are possessing a light recessive gene and a dark dominant progressive gene which produce light and dark complected black people. This creation mirrored in Illumini (the light) and Atom's existence in them. Now Illumini is translated in this physical realm as light and consciousness or the ability to say I am. It was meant to be peaceful at first but that was until this universe entrapped it into violent happenings now there is an unstable happening every time there were new entities birthed. The instability became eventually the unravelling, and because they began entrapping, this is for what it's worth. The Dark man and women once ruled this world with an elegant heir of extravagance. Their seed were the developers of science, art, music, the writers of history and creators of mathematics. They built elegant and extravagant kingdoms all over the land. Their land, Ham names after Adham would be located where Africa and the middle east are today. The richest part of the planet in terms of natural resources, in this rich region in which they were created, they thrived and all around the planet they began to expand, establish kingdoms and set up governments some that still stand to this day.

The Return of the Dark People Vol. 5: 'The Days of DOGUN and the Lumni'

Black people dominated and ruled the world for millions of centuries, with wealth and power that everyone could experience, everything that could be attained came to them in plenty it seemed that they were destined to see a celestial kingdom come and their knowledge of the power of Atom was their deliverance. That was until the days of Dr. Dogun, a scientist the most prolific, a theologist the most accurate, and a professor of many subjects if there was any man close to being a God he was it, in his days there wasn't a man smarter all around the world tribes looked and found none, he healed the weak and sick. He owned the world's scientific and historic library and it was also the largest, he held peace prizes and honorable accolades for his work he was a genius among his people. If there ever was a catastrophic problem he would be the one to solve it. But at times he would get greedy with his knowledge, arrogant almost to the point of pure evil. You see he figured out that we were here for a divine reason we were to leave this dimension. We were the sequel to who he viewed and called the Dark People. The knowledge that man was physical matter was something that the governments of the world was not yet ready for, but the knowledge was found in his library. The plan was to build a machine that would decode the atoms in human bodies there for transforming their physical nature into something other than what we see as physical caption and then there were was more that he had in store. The world's governments were against this, and there broke a feud between the two. One side saying this was unnatural and the other saying this is a natural truth. The government shut him down and ceased all of his statistics and work. His library he purchased with his enormous wealth all of his inventions and awards were gone and left him bitter with no possessions. He was left with the notion to retaliate for what it was all worth. Dogun though was formidable in the mainstream world, he had followers of all kind, man, woman, boy, and girl. They purchased weapons and began to blow up government embassies all over the world. He and some of his followers were eventually caught, tried, convicted, and exiled to an island in the upper cooler region on the planet, which would eventually work to his advantage. You see he knew that the majority of black people fail to realize about themselves. That they had two different genes that produces light and dark pigment. With over 200,000 followers he began mating the lightest complected with lightest complected producing lighter skinned people until eventually, years later there were a race of pale beings that were designed to bring upon black people, destruction and death. Dogun though had one up on everybody that exiled him, he was able to store the history of all man's knowledge and history on one strand about the size of a small rope. In which he would teach to his Lumini race (called that and derived from the ancient term Illumini meaning light) and form armies throughout the European regions to spread and conquer and leave bloody and bleeding was his only hope... gather them to Africa, overtake and replace the dark human race. At least that was the original plight, that began to float. Dogun was up in age in these days and now the race of beings that he created began to sense weakness in him, so they plotted to have he and his family assassinated, new leadership was needed, so they thought, to complete them. Many centuries passed and then it was time to infiltrate black people they started at the very heart of the land. They took over and mass murdered millions with false religion, other tribes that they couldn't physically conquer, they pitted against one another creating a chain reaction genocide killing a couple billion, a black eye for all of man.

The Return of the Dark People Vol. 6: Enslaved and Recolonised

Now the Lumini were a ruthless race set on the notion of divide and conquer, once they had grown in number, they infiltrated the world's politics and religious and school systems and set the destruction of the dominant race to a freefall at an extraordinary pace. Destroying the ancients' libraries and killing off all of the scholars and priest who taught the religions of Adham and mirrored in Eve, Illuminis being of peace. Being that they had all of mankind's knowledge and history once they colonised on every continent their basic intent was to deprive upcoming generations of this knowledge and it became lost and talks of it became a mystery and they began to bring the reign of Dark people to an end. Now the

Lumini could not believe that the dark people were the basis of everything, even though the evidence was right there in the dark people themselves. Not all of them were this dogmatic about how we came into being there were a band of Lumini people who had a heart and for the dark people they felt. Seeing the brutal mass killings of billions of people made many of them realize as to why it seemed that they had no soul but the dark people did and the fact that a once peaceful race was being destroyed and enslaved just showed that the Lumini were truly evil. It was this way until the days in which there came the prophecy of En 2000 centuries in after the enslavement began.

The Return of the Dark People Vol. 7: "The Prophecy of EN"

There was a wealthy tribe of dark people off of the southwest coast of Africa who were an exception to the captivity rule. They were free because of the way that they have mastered how to interpret dreams, their pineal gland produces more melanin than most tribes and this allows them to see into the fourth dimension and their knowledge of the cosmos were just some of their abilities and things that they were able to do. The Lumini were fearful and wanted nothing to do, as far as war goes, with the Nibiru. Instead, they tried to use them for their own benefit looking to befriend them as long as they can because they knew that they could rally the dark race of people who remain under Lumini control around the world and could not break through. The leader of the Nibiru, Lutheran received an epiphany or an energetic vision if you will and a prophecy from EN, the energy inside every black man and woman, the inner soul or sun in which all life is connected, , he stated that Energy would return to prominence and dominate once they realize their will, who they are and what lives within and accept it, because that is where they come from. Now En would not return in the form of a physical man, but energy in the minds of the ones who were deprived because of the Lumini, to bring their children back to the celestial kingdom. This was Illumini's plan. Being that En was already entrapped inside of man he was energized by his mother's plight to bring he and his siblings back into the spiritual land. Starting with the mind and then on into the rest of the body, En was ignited and dispersed into the people who began this planet the dark skinned seed of Adham who started to believe that they could come up out of it. Now the Lumini are feeling damned. The dark people are becoming rowdy as they began to orchestrate music to build confidence. They get ready to seize the Lumini's plan of destruction and diffuse it, they becoming reluctant to their opposers and now united under a flowing unstoppable EN, it's now evidence of their captivity, and without evidence seen, they hoped for things of great substance; thus showcasing the all mighty faith in the face of the formidable Illumini who recognized her children in Adham's seed and brought back to their memory of how to get back. Back to the true reality and back to substance. This matter that we are in right now is an illusion, a mere creation outside of the original creator's truth and actuality. We are the proof of the dark people's existence. The Lumini are aware of this but do not know that the way back is through the original beings who began with this planet, their effort to destroy and to take over is shown in their quest for absolute power showcasing that in their persistence searching for new ways to bring more fatalities. But plans were in the works by some of the Lumini governments to free the dark people and give them rights. Despite the plight, there were some, who are also becoming the majority, who realized that the way to absolute power went through the original man and the plan was theirs to orchestrate and bring the glory.

The Return of the Dark People Vol. 8: "A New Era"

In the days after the prophecy of EN was fulfilled their dawned a new era. With many different colors, creeds, cultures, and races all over the land, there was a new message that needed to be instilled, how to get a back to infinite dominance and this would begin with a war on terror. The Lumini was now not a race of people, but a secret sect, who knew of the powers of the dark people and now operated under other names, orchestrating wars and catastrophes within other races of people controlling the financial, religious, and economic systems covering up their great unjust but looking at us useful projects.

The Return of the Dark People Vol. 9: "The Value of Melanin"-The Substance

Now melanin was the basic and most powerful component in existence. In the cosmos, it is the combination of black energy and dark matter illuminated by love between the female passive material forces of the Illumini and the active energetic forces of the Atom. It is a constant sexual play the passion for each other gives them creative focus, and the attraction is such that they can resist it. And so as the creation story goes, the Illumini virginity broken and now she is separated into three sides, the highs of the skies and space, the lows of the oceans, seas, rivers, and lakes, and the third and highest, most potent form reside in the black man the first man and the culmination of the absolute. You've seen his face. The triple darkness of space. The very power that is life in this universe, the seed, the light or magical child, the atom or Adham from the Illumini. To him and his dark people who are now just using 10% of themselves to try and find their way back to that celestial and infinite place where no physicality can entrap their amazing grace, that is a sight for their sore eyes. Now is the time to look up into the sky and see within yourselves and retrieve that other 90% of your capacity because that is your natural place. But beware the Lumini are a devil race looking for any chance to still your melanin and use it to build theirs up make theirs the ace. They want to replace us with themselves so to keep that from happening we must look within and remember who we are, that is the only way the dark people can give us help. The kingdom that they know of has to come from within, as shown from the miraculous conception of the atom from the Illumini then vise-versa and creation began. Knowing the whole story of the dark people, these are the things that the lumini have kept from the dark man. Knowing the powers of the melanin and how it translates to God's immaculate master plan. The combination of the absolute, the female forces, woman and the male forces, man. This is God himself. The black family and the division of that family proceeds the destruction which is how they came to power in the first place by destroying and raping the family to death, and separating the woman from the man.

The Return of the Dark People Vol. 10: "Accessing the Power"

The power was melanin and a melanin coated people as strong as good and evil combined was the melanin intertwined with the formidable forces of the cosmic dust, which produced us in the form of the hue-mans and eventually mankind. We put the hue in hueman with the highest most potent form of the melanin, which gave birth to the triple darkness of space, residing in us. We are the proof in what they say can't be proven. That there is a God and they live in us. Trust that the dark people will return, when we deepen the hue of our souls to crimson, dark red and let it burn as the cosmic dust, the Earth. Our thinking can sink deeper than the oceans or levitate higher than midnight universe but, only when we access the powers of the hue and do what comes natural to us, potent but unnatural to those who lack that and view. Release the voodoo and access the powers of the dark only then will blackmagic do what it is destined to do seek, kill, and destroy, play its powerful part.

The Return Of The Dark People Vol. 11: "The Return To Grace"

Melanin is the most powerful; substance in all of existence, the cosmic glue that holds our universe and reality together. Its possibilities are fueled by truth and are limitless and the only way to achieve immortality and live forever. Known as the Kah which are our different levels of consciousness and so is where the word comes from. Melanin or the substance is in everything. It is carbon and is the source in which we all come from. It is known as the leftover remnants of the GODs of the ancient world before man and mankind existed. Entrapped and embodied into a 3 dimensional being, the Dark People became the conscious of everything that exists. The melanin or the substance is sought out by the evil lumini so that if they can harness it they would, then use it to achieve this power of immortality. You see they lack abundance of the substance and cannot generate enough energy to refuel, recharge, and rebuild their physical and psychological being and capacity. The substance is a gateway between the physical and spiritual world. It is absolute power, natural and unnatural all at the same time and was taught to be an agent of evil by the lumini in order to detour the Dark People from tapping into the dark powers and truth about their origins of the miraculous birth, because of the melanin which is the pigment of the Dark people and the universe. The black race had an insight and that the lumini did not possess. They were able to receive En (Energy) through the sunlight which empowers the melanin and they began to vibrate on a higher frequency, thus being able to control Matt (material) and Space on the Earth. These powers they would soon learn to test.

The Return Of The Dark People Vol. 12: "Energy, The Inner Sun"

The source of all life and creation was melanin. The substance was darkness and light which translates to knowledge and wisdom. If there was an order in the universe, this is the order that they fell in matter, energy, space, and time, all intertwined with our souls and conscious, the remnants of the Gods who lived before us, before we became this third dimensional creation. The combination of the illuminate energy and the atom and dark matter the Illumini, which is material, miraculously birth the energy of the atom. And so you see the creation is immaculate. As compacted melanin or matter explodes into pure light and thus the stars are born, thus producing life. This process also happens on the terrestrial plane. As we are made of melanin, and when compacted together we birth a flame and explosion of pure light which is the inner sun the connector, and binder of all conscious life, it is the remnants of the ancient world before the physical, the melanin reigns supreme in physical flesh. The pineal gland in our brains produces melanin and gives us extraordinary powers. Thus which is why the lumini hate us and our melanin they want to extract for themselves and devour. We are immortal, light existing in a dark body just as the stars and universe before them. The substance in which they seek it holds powers beyond belief which is why the lumini yearn to explore them, but the return of the DARK PEOPLE are poised to sublime, the beginning is birth from the ending, thus the release of the first and last one, Chronos, and now it is time. I'm the powerful perfect product and result of the mix between good and evil. So are all of you, if you believe in THE RETURN OF THE DARK PEOPLE.

About The Author

I, Timothy Vonce-Waylon Lane was born to my parents, Luther T. Lane and Vanessa G. Lane on July 26, 1978 in Dallas, Tx. Raised with a southern baptist christian background I always knew that there was more to the story, to my story, to our story. I spent my whole life wandering and wondering about dark places. When I realized that greatness comes out of Africa I was maybe 11 or 12 years old. My father was in sales and my mother was a registered nurse and they always brought me back to that foundation of greatness. They both exceled at their occupation, and by providing for me and my sister they showed us both the value of persistence and hard work. I had humble beginnings as I began in the rough Southern Oak Cliff area as a child. When I was about 9 years old my mother and father moved in together and we made our home in the suburban area of the Dallas sector a then small town called

Cedar Hill. I graduated from Cedar Hill High School in 1996 and I attended Navarro College before coming home and attending the local El Centro Community College in Dallas. It was around this time when I was diagnosed with schyzophrenia and my college education was halted. I never went back. However, I took it upon myself to educate myself on my condition as well as the mental and spiritual condition of myself and my people and I found that the majority of us are really in a bad mental and spiritual state. So I decided to write a book describing, well, at least my mental and spiritual state and the very things and issues that formed them. I met and fell in love with who I describe as Queen of Queens my children's mother Mahogany Byrd. She has been my strength in all of this. It takes a strong person to live with someone with mental illness, and she is the strongest. I could not have created this without her. Her and my three children are the reason why I do this. I am truly blessed and fortunate to be in a position where I can help someone whether you are mentally ill yourself or know someone who is mentally ill or even if you are not affected but you just lack a little spiritual direction, truth is always the best fulfiller, there is never anything deeper or anything realer.